A Way with Horses

Prologue

A person needs someone to believe in him. A horse has this need too. Whether the horse is bred to race, show-jump, hunt, or hack, he needs some one to recognise his heart and courage, and his power to perform. This person may be his owner or trainer, but sometimes it is his jockey, rider or groom. But in any case, it is this individual who forms a partnership with the horse and has the uncanny ability to turn a giddy three year old or obstreperous mare or gelding into a champion. It is through this person's patience, firmness mixed with kindness, and penchant to routine that races are won, Grand Prix are lifted and country is crossed.

Niamh O'Dochartaigh has chosen ten individuals or families from Galway who have spent their lives forming such partnerships with horses and ponies. She has talked to these people and tried to come up with an understanding of what makes these partnerships so rewarding and successful. Each one of these people, whose lives revolve around horses, finds a special sort of satisfaction in living this type of life-style and gives inspiration to the rest of us horse-lovers to try to do the same.

Kate McMahon
American-born children's author and resident of Galway since 1980

Contents

Contents

Preface

What kind of people choose to build a major part of their lives around the sounds, sights and athletic abilities of the horse, one of modern man's most valued domestic animals?

The answer lies in the simple truth that there is no one particular type of horse-person, but that there are many different varieties of people who enjoy being with and working with horses and who regularly participate in different sporting activities with them. By talking with some of these people I have tried to provide a little understanding of the mindset that finds such immense satisfaction in the long hours of work and activity involved in the care and company of their horse or pony.

Since first domesticated sometime pre-2000 BC, the horse has been the most admired four-legged animal in the world. In Irish mythology the horse is often referred to as being worthy only of the Gods, that is, too noble in bearing and in stature for mere human use. But as the human race evolved and horses became valuable primarily as food, men discovered that this wild creature might be useful to them in ways other than as meat to be hunted and killed. Captured and tamed, the wild horse of the plains, with its incredible speed of movement and ability to cover great distances — combined with its hardiness and a biddable nature — soon became a necessary ally in man's desire to travel, to explore and to conquer new territories.

Workhorse and Warhorse

Because *equus* is basically a creature of the wild open plains and mountains, a flight animal, programmed to flee the approach of the long extinct predator, its natural place in life is with the family herd. In modern times, this herd existence, which meant horses were constantly on the move, grazing long hours over a wide expanse of territory,

ears ever pricked and alert to sounds of danger, bonding and breeding the young of the next generation, is in danger of extinction.

The natural herd life no longer exists for many horses. Nowadays we humans invariably keep them in artificial conditions, often alone, in fields or in stables, and we have kept the horse in this unnatural way for centuries. Nonetheless the modern-day lifestyle of the horse is far superior to that endured by many working animals even up to the mid-twentieth century. In earlier years the horse was, for the most part, both a beast of burden and a beast of war, pulling heavy loads, carrying men and armaments into bloody battles and dying in its thousands through overwork and neglect on city streets or in the horrible maelstrom of the battlefield. Even as late as 1939 the infamous charge of the Polish cavalry against German tanks resulted in a horrendous bloodbath of thousands of men and horses at the commencement of World War Two. A huge number of these Warhorses were purchased at Irish Fairs down through the centuries. Horses working on farms, although working hard all year round, possibly had a healthier and better life.

The Leisure Horse

In modern times, since the end of that last War in Europe, that recent phenomenon, the Leisure Horse, has arrived. Liberated from the shackles of heavy and unsuitable work, the horse now enjoys a much freer existence than formerly. Well fed, cared for, exercised, freed from the confines of its comfortable stable for long periods in the field in the company of other horses, it may well enjoy a lifestyle closer to that of its wild-horse ancestor; with the added bonus of extra feeding when necessary. Yet the natural herd characteristics remain an integral part of the nature of even the most domesticated and placid horse or pony. Just as in the herd, a natural order of leader and follower

applies. In the horse-human bond, the human always holds the dominant role while the horse is always subordinate, dependant on man for his food, recreation and general welfare. Basically man dominates, and is responsible for, the horse's whole existence.

Horses are undoubtedly domesticated, but not in the same way as a dog or cat is tame, house trained, a constant companion to their owner, usually petted, pampered and treated almost as one of the family. These herd animals with their youngsters playing together, occasionally fearful of unfamiliar sights or sounds, biting and kicking among themselves or repelling a newcomer to the herd, are in all respects a race apart from the family dog or cat. Perhaps it is some aspect of this combination of wildness and tameness in the horse character that attracts and maintains such a mesmeric hold over many individuals of the human race, individuals who are, themselves, a race apart in the human family. It is evident that the large unblinking eye of the horse, seen at close quarters, seems to have a captivating effect on even the youngest of children, and many are captives for life of this enigmatic spell.

The Horse People

The horse-people in this book are horse-lovers who empathise with their charges but not in a sentimental or maudlin way. An appreciation of the beauty and quality of this fine looking creature is indeed a major part of the attraction. These horse-minders are entranced by the very appearance of an animal of good conformation and movement. They will see beauty in the movement and stance of the horse, even simply in the way they change coat and colour with the seasons, and they will also recognise and appreciate the different character traits seen in each individual horse.

At the same time they show practical consideration in the way they care for their charges, aware of their material needs, feeding, mucking out when they are stabled, and grooming them. Right through training, teaching and riding them, the human masters are continuously striving to attain a partnership between horse and human where each will thrive and grow under the influence of the other. The people involved seem to develop a shared sense of humour, apparently connected to their dealings with this most enchanting of all creatures. They realise that these animals will, on the good days, exceed all expectations for their riders or owners and on bad days may behave so erratically that the sense of humour is the only appropriate satisfactory human reaction or response. Above all each one of them really likes and respects horses and wants only the best for them.

The people portrayed in these pages are not famous or even well known outside their immediate circles of family, friends and other competitors in their chosen sport or lifestyle. They are simply ordinary Galway people, known to me, whose lives revolve around horses. Look for their like in any County in Ireland and you will find them.

Pencil sketches above, by Eavan O'Dochartaigh

Horse's head by Eavan O'Dochartaigh

Acknowledgements

Forever in my memory will remain the friendship and help of the following individuals who all shared a common love-the love of Horses.

Family members Eoin, Eavan and Aideen who read the chapters as they materialised and also Eavan for the sketches and artwork she supplied.

Garnet Irwin, RIP Spring 2005, and Ruth Cully, who allowed me to use the old Irwin family pictures; and Nicola Musgrave, Willie Barry and Pat White who shared memories on the family .

Michael Tully and Chick Gillen provided a fund of information and stories of times past in Galway.

Eamon O'Donohue was happy to recall his childhood days in Galway of the nineteen forties and his Army Show-jumping experience.

Bobby and Bridget Bolger shared stories of their Connemara Pony experiences and Championship winning ways.

Shirley North graciously gave me time and the use of her many photos and newspapers cuttings.

Tomás and Frances O'Brien gave pictures and stories of the family's Show-jumping fortunes.

Judy Cazabon provided an insight both into her life spent running a Riding Centre and the family's Show Ring involvement.

Val O'Brien shared information both on the good times and the problems involved in running a National Hunt Trainer's Yard and from Lorna Murphy came the lady Jockey's view.

In the Hardiman family thanks are due to Sean and Maura, Marjorie and Mark Field, and Bernard, Eleanor and Shauna Finneran, who gave me new insights into Riding Clubs and Dressage.

Lisa Rodgers, Design and Layout artist was always cheerful and positive in coping with my various shortcomings and computer inadequacies.

A special thank you to Deacy & Associates, Chartered Accountants and Elwood Office Interiors, for contributing to publishing costs.

Niamh O'Dochartaigh

Chapter 1

*Garnet aged 14 with first ponies **Rob** and **Starlight***

Garnet Irwin
1913-2005

An old lady looks back

In a nursing- home just outside Cleggan in north west Connemara, an old lady with clear blue eyes sat in her armchair, knitting. She gazed out on the strand below her window, noted the colour and condition of the sea today and smiled when she remembered her past exploits on this and other strands in this westerly outpost she called home. For it was in this area that Garnet Irwin, the young tomboy, as she was known then, flew free on her beloved horses and was to become a legendry horsewoman, many years ago and in a different world.

Civil War and poverty
Cleggan is only a short distance from Ross House, Moyard, where Garnet lived for most of her life since she was a young child, when her father, Alfred Irwin, settled here in 1919 and became the local doctor. He had served four years as an army major in France during the Great War. The war veteran was returning home, to the town-land by the Atlantic, where his father, Benjamin Irwin was rector in the Anglican Church of St. Thomas, Moyard, in the parish of Ballinakill. Garnet spoke of the appalling poverty in the area in the early years and of her father's care and affection for the sick and poor and of his reputation as a gentle man, giving his medical services impartially, wherever he was needed, especially during the bitter Civil War years.

The early years at Ross were exciting ones for the Irwin children. The Civil War, or 'the bad times' as she called that period, meant that Republican and Free State forces were at each other's throats. An early memory is of her mother Muriel, holding back some Free State men at the hall door as her father patched up a bullet wound on a young I.R.A

man in a back room of the house, and the family hoping that he would escape before the house was searched. She described that area of Ballinakill Bay as a bolt-hole, where it was easy to hop in a boat and row to Letter across the bay.

Dr. Irwin did many house-calls as part of his work, first in the pony and trap and later in his old car. This early model of transport had a tendency to suffer headlamp failure on the darkest nights, which necessitated his helper having to walk in front of the car to light the way along the track with the lamp, which was always kept in readiness for such an emergency. Tuberculosis was a deadly plague of that era and Dr. Irwin is remembered today for his heroic endeavours to minister to the sick and needy with skill and tenderness, rarely receiving payment. A neighbour, Willie Barry, who lived next door, worked for the Irwin family for many years, as did his father before him: in fact both Dr. Alfred and Willie's father both received medals for war services. Willie speaks of the doctor as 'a gentle man, much loved and respected,' one who never shirked the stormy trips to Inisbofin Island to visit the sick, even, on one occasion, with his broken arm in a sling as a result of a shooting accident.

Ross House
Ross House, on the shores of Ballinakill Bay, has an impressive high archway which leads into the old stableyard. Part of the building had served as a coastguard lookout in the early 19th century and for some years it was occupied by a Thomas Prior who is remembered as a harsh landlord. He is said to have ordered that a woman be tarred and feathered for stealing a turnip! These were not tranquil times in this isolated part of the country.

Irwin family at Ross House, 1929. Father Alfred, Garnet with dog, mother Muriel with small friend, Betty Marchant, Harry's wife. In front brother Harry.

*Dr. Alfred Irwin, Garnet's father, riding **Spaniard**, 1912.*

Shanboolard gate. Garnet at centre back, Nell Duane standing centre and Pam Tulloch.

*A riding party at Cleggan Farm. Graham Tulloch on **Morning Star**, Betty Marchant on **Foxglove**, Nell Duane on **Starlight**, Pam Tulloch on **Pricilla**, and Kay Fisher on **Daisy**.*

The O'Flaherty chieftains had ruled most of Connemara between the 13th and 17th centuries, until Galway merchant families, notably the Martins, gradually bought them out. As a result of the depredations of the Cromwellian regime in the mid 17th century the remaining O'Flaherty Chiefs were either hanged or expropriated and the Martins held ownership of the largest Estate in either England or Ireland, for two centuries.

However, it was the Lynchs of Bearna, some four miles west of Galway, who held the land around Ballinakill Bay and in 1843 they sold the estate of over 10,000 acres, which contained Ross and other large houses, to a Robert Graham of Keelkyle. Fifty years later, William Armstrong Lushington Tulloch bought the house and it was his wife Kate who sold it to the Irwins.

Most of the land had been acquired by the congested Districts Board by 1921 for division among the tenants, but a sufficient acreage to support a small farm had been left with Ross House. The spacious farm outbuildings included three unused granaries, relics of former land agent occupation. Its commodious yard and stables suited Garnet admirably and she was to lead many a winner under the Ross House archway in her heyday as a jockey competing in the Connemara races.

The Church of Ireland Community

There was a thriving Anglo-Irish Church of Ireland community — most of whom had served in the foreign service — in this sector of north Connemara at the time. Garnet recalled with admiration Kate Armstrong Lushington Tulloch, of Shanbolard Hall, whose early married-life had been spent on a log-cabin ranch in Wyoming, raising large numbers of cattle and breeding horses. One story tells of this formidable, taffata-clad, lady lying out on the prairie at night with a

rifle, guarding her horses from the Indians! This was indeed the wild west of the 1880s. This lady was a skilful driver of any type of horse-drawn conveyance and a regular winner of driving classes at Agricultural Shows, including the Connacht Grand Provincial Horse Show in Galway's Eyre Square. It was from her that Garnet first learned to ride and was also given as a gift, an injured foal that her doctor father had stitched up and saved.

First pony — Rob

When Kate Tulloch gave her grandfather, the rector, a Welsh cob named *Rob* to pull his trap, this was a real beginning. *Rob* in time became Garnet's responsibility, and thus started a passion that was to remain close to her heart for the rest of her life. On the steady black cob she explored the country lanes and the strands of north Connemara, often travelling many miles from home. These peregrinations were a cause of anxiety to her English born mother Muriel, who was not at all familiar with horses, yet she never prevented her adventurous daughter from independently going her own way and for this Garnet was ever-grateful. Muriel knew that her only daughter was passionately attached to her ponies and was happiest when out riding her mounts in the lonely countryside or looking after them in the yard at home.

After early home schooling she became a weekly boarder at Kylemore Abbey. She loved her schooldays with the Benedictine nuns and remained friendly with some of the sisters in her later years. A year at finishing school in England followed and then it was home and horses full-time. Her two brothers, Pat and Harry, went off to University and qualified as an engineer and a doctor respectively, but Garnet — after her initial plan to become a vet was discouraged — stayed on in the family home, reading all she could get hold of on the training and care of horses and soon

5th form at Kylemore Abbey School 1929.

With tennis coach Miss Slingsly, St. Zita's Finishing School near Bournmouth, England, 1931

*With **Wickford**, **Swallow** and **Rob** (aged 31) at Ross entrance arch 1931*

*Garnet on **Bess**, Hugh on **Ginger**, and Mary on **Betty** riding at Sellerna beach in 1930.*

*Garnet holds **Fair Thistle** by the Thoroughbred stallion **Thistleton ex Foxglove**. The Thoroughbred-Native pony cross was used to produce suitable animals for the popular flapper-racing in Connemara.*

*With **Swallow** at Clifden Races 1932.*

horses and ponies became her whole life, 'all I ever wanted to do'.

She was brought to the first Pony Show in Roundstone organised by the newly formed Connemara Pony Breeders Society in 1924 and the great excitement of a cow with triplet calves, which attracted huge crowds stood out in her memory. Since that first Show she attended every Connemara Pony Show for about sixty years and also served on the Council of the Society for twenty years from 1961-1981. She remembered, as a girl, riding to the Show in Carna in south Connemara, taking several days to complete the round trip of some sixty miles, often alone but sometimes, in later years, accompanied by a younger friend Ann Tulloch.

She took part in trial gallops at Shanboolard and rode to Omey and other beaches with friends. Care and knowledge of the tides was always necessary for a trip to Omey as here, across the wide expanse of sand separating the mainland from Omey island, the tide floods in with startling speed, and many a picnic and riding excursion had to end swiftly as the seas surged forward. These were the carefree summer days of the tranquil Thirties between wars, spent riding with cousins and friends, fishing and bathing, or walking the dogs; a privileged group of people at ease with themselves and the world. After *Rob* other ponies and later part-breds and thoroughbreds came through her yard and racing became an important part of her life.

Pony Racing and Flapping

Her first introduction to pony racing was at the Clifden track, based at Curvoghill grounds east of the town. She asked her father if any of his patients there had a pony they might let her ride in the final race of the day, the Visitors Plate which was confined to riders who had not raced earlier. Neighbour Festy Barry obliged and Garnet hopped

on to the tiny chestnut mare which tore off, flat out, and won the race, much to her young rider's surprise.

After that she was hooked and her mother bought her a bigger well-bred pony, a part-thoroughbred named Swallow, from a Mrs Lavelle who had found the mare a little hot to manage. Then began her participation in flapper racing in earnest, the sport that was to absorb all her energies. Swallow never won but was always placed. Local racing pundits said her rider was too kind, 'ah, you never used your stick miss'.

In the mornings she rode and schooled her own horses and the afternoons were spent training and riding out young animals belonging to neighbours. She became known as a brilliant jockey much admired for her riding exploits and owners often asked her to ride races for them, to which she always agreed. Riding some of the half-trained ponies on beaches was no easy matter, as you had to make a sharp turn at each end of the strand and turning a pony with an unmade mouth could mean ending up in the sea or on the rocks if you were unlucky.

Garnet often rode horses and ponies for neighbour Matt Duane, and recalled one of these horses in particular which was bought for five pounds at the Dublin Spring Show and afterwards raced successfully with Garnet as *Irish Lady*. Among her many racing honours she won the Cleggan Plate in 1935 aboard Mr. Joyce's *Rainbow*, who was by the thoroughbred sire *Thistleton*. The racetrack was the mecca for horses and ponies of that era and much thoroughbred blood was introduced to improve the size and the speed of the native pony. The thoroughbred *Thistleton*, who stood with Christy Kerins in Oranmore, was a favoured sire to put to the Connemara mare to produce a winner on the track. Garnet also trained and rode her own

Garnet's brothers, Pat and Harry Irwin

*Pat's polo ponies, **Cavalier** and **Mary**, with grooms in India 1932*

*Preparing to race **Swallow** at Clifden Races1932, with mother Muriel and father Alfred.*

*Pat with polo pony **Mary** in India.*

horses and ponies at the many race meetings in the Connemara area, both on strands and on improvised tracks, during the nineteen thirties and forties when her own *Wickford*, a thoroughbred by *Retreat*, was a favourite on the circuit.

Omey strand, Roundstone's Gurteen strand, Lettergesh beach near Tully Cross and Clifden racecourse-where the holiday village is today-were some of the tracks where Garnet raced and often won. As Muriel had no transport, she often waited anxiously at home when her daughter rode off to a race meeting, knowing that Garnet would be racing hell-for-leather in the middle of a group of rough boy-riders whose sole instruction from owners was — according to Garnet — 'watch Garnet Irwin and get rid of her if you can'.

Her mother had good cause to worry, especially when Clifden was the racing venue.

Nicola Musgrave's mother Ann Tulloch, a grand-daughter of the legendary Kate, was a friend and racing companion of Garnet. Nicola tells of an old ruin on the far side of the Clifden course behind which horses were obliterated for a minute from the watching crowds. This provided an opportunity for some unsporting riding practice, such as moving close enough to the girl rider to try to get a foot under the stirrup in an effort to dislodge the female competition, all part and parcel of the rough and tumble sport of the day. However, Garnet survived, unbowed, and in twenty five years she was lucky enough to get away with only one single fall, and she 'lived for those races, they were great fun'.

As a young woman, racing was her first and only love, 'all so long ago, a job I loved doing, but great fun and sometimes illegal', and in Garnet's world these were the halcyon days. She had little interest in dressing-up and socialising and practically lived in her riding clothes. It has been suggested that it was because she adored and respected her father to such an extent that other men did not live up to her high expectations and in the event she never married.

Showing and Breeding

When the popularity of racing waned, Connemara pony breeding and showing became of greater interest to her and she bred her first Connemara foal in 1938. In time she became motorised and acquired a second-hand trailer which she pulled all over the county, bumping along the potholed tracks and travelling to Races and to Shows as far from home as Oughterard, Ballinasloe and Dublin.

Camlin was the prefix Garnet chose for the Connemara ponies she bred and they were regular winners at Clifden and Dublin Shows for many years. Her foundation mare, *Camlin Ciro*, won ten red rosettes at Clifden between 1949 and 1962. At the 1953 Connemara Pony Show, Ciro and her daughter *Camlin Cilla* took home both the Killannin and the Archbishop's cups. On board *Ciro* Garnet won the first Class for ridden Connemara ponies organised by the Spring Show at the R.D.S. in 1951. *Ciro* also won show-jumping events with rider Margaret McCartan, and competed successfully in jumping competitions against novice horses and is reputed to have jumped a five foot wall at Castlebar Show with Garnet as jockey! *Ciro* was the only foal of Garnet's former racing mare Swallow and was by the Connemara stallion Silver Pearl.

Cannonball

It was during the late nineteen sixties and early seventies when Garnet was a Connacht representative of the fledgling Irish Pony Society that she wrote an entertaining Yearbook article on *Cannon Ball*. This famous stallion, unbeaten on the racetrack, the grand-son of a Welsh Cob sire and a

*Desmond Duane with Thoroughbred **Irish Lady** at Omey Races 1933.*

***Swallow** and Garnet in racing mode August 1935.*

*With her Connemara mare **Camlin Ciro**, Swallow's only foal, by the Connemara Stallion Silver Pearl, Garnet won the 1st Ridden Connemara Class which was held at the Spring Show at Dublin's RDS.in 1951.*

*Garnet's home-bred **Little Camlin** winning one of many Ridden Hunter Classes at Ballinrobe Show 1957.*

Racing at Omey Strand, 2003

native mare, was the Number One stallion in the Stud Book of the Connemara Pony Breeders Society in 1923. Garnet as a child had heard all the stories his fame had generated and was actually at the 'wake' as described in her article. She had an indelible memory of him when she wrote this piece forty six years after his death in 1926 and had she followed her writing bent she might perhaps have made a name for herself in the literary world in her later years.

Much as she admired *Cannon Ball*, she claimed that the best and most productive input to the breed came with the introduction of *Carna Dun*. By the thoroughbred, *Little Heaven*, who was introduced by the Society into Connemara in 1947, *Carna Dun* was subsequently the sire of Tommy Wade's brilliant show-jumper *Dundrum* who 'wowed' the world in the fifties, and of *Little Model* who reached Grand Prix level in Dressage. These names, Garnet believed, had put the Connemara Pony on the world map and were the reason for the popularity of the native pony to this day. It angered her to think of how *Little Heaven* was disposed of in the end, being sold at Athenry cattle fair to a dealer for nine pounds, and transported to England for the meat trade.

At Ross the Irwin family bred about two foals each year and, as the land was limited and they also kept some cattle, the colts were sold on and only the fillies were kept. The mare *Cilla* produced the colt *Camlin Cicada* and the filly *Camlin Capella*, both by *Carna Dun*. In later years Ann Tulloch and her friend Evelyn Holberton would ride from Cleggan over to Ross, meeting Garnet halfway, usually riding 'something buzzy', with her headscarf wrapped round her head in turban style and sporting her 'elephant ears jodhpurs', and they would ride out together, to Ard Kyle or some other nearby strand.

Later Life

Although not of the majority Catholic religion, Garnet disclaimed the idea that there was ever any discrimination towards herself or her family or that she ever felt an outsider in this remote area of Connemara. Her dad, she said, was loved by the people and although her mother took her on occasional trips to London to visit her branch of the family, and they went to plays and films there and they certainly adored the Royal family, she was always happy to return to Ross as the land and the countryside were very dear to her. She was a devout church- goer and loyal to her Anglican tradition and to St. Thomas's church in Moyard where her Irwin forbears had served as rectors. She looked after her parents until they died in the 1970s and buried them among the ancestors in the quiet graveyard in this area of unspoilt natural grandeur.

In the late seventies and soon after her parents died she was left a legacy consisting of an old farmhouse and some land in California. She didn't like the new Ireland that she suspected was going to turn to Communism. So she sold Ross House, sold all her tack, rugs and belongings, had her cats and dogs humanely put down, and headed off to make a new life for herself, first to England and then on to America to what she expected to be her own 'little house on the prairie'.

However, the U.S. venture did not work out as planned and the ageing Garnet found her legacy rapidly disappearing into legal pockets, and she returned finally to settle near her home place in the mid 1980s and to grow old, with only her dogs and her vivid memories of good times gone by to sustain her, a fine lady with a wondrous past.

Cannon Ball *with owner Henri Toole, sketch from photo by Jay Murphy.*

A Pony in a Thousand
(Cannon Ball No 1, Vol 1, C.P.S.B.)

Cannon Ball and I were both four-year-olds when we first met. Twice a year for the next twenty years, at Easter and in the Summer, we renewed our friendship.

Cannon Ball was a Connemara pony, but not one of those rough, shaggy little chaps you see anywhere from Galway to the coast, hauling turf, working "on the road" when farming is slack, or taking the family to Mass on Sundays in the side-car, though he did all those tasks-and pulled a plough as well. By some trick of nature he was born, if not bred, an aristocrat. The snow-white of his coat, the proud carriage of his head, the short back and the splendid muscle of his quarters raised him above the level of his kind in life, and, in death, made him a legend..

Perhaps you have seen the Prince Eugene monument in the Heldenplatz in Vienna. The Prince rides a true Lippizaner horse, with a pedigree going back to the sixteenth century. *Cannon Ball* might have been that mount.

Our holidays were spent in a lodge hard by the Galway-Clifden road, midway between Oughterard and Maam Cross. The first Wednesday of the month was fair day in Oughterard. At eight o'clock on Fair Day the road below the lodge would ring with the sounds of hoofs and we would glimpse the white pony, pulling the cart (if Pat Toole John was taking in sheep or a bullock) or the side-car, if it was just a matter of eggs and the monthly carousal. The village was full of Tooles, Pat Tooles in particyular, and it was said locally that it was the last place on earth God made, so he left his tools there. Anyway, it was necessary to suffix the Christian name of the father in order to tell one Pat Toole from another.

Whichever the vehicle selected, the return journey followed an invariable pattern. As the sun sank low behind the Ttwelve Pins of Connemara to the westward, the hoofs would ring out again and *Cannon Ball* would spank by the lodge, ears pricked, forelegs a poem of movement; but of driver there would be no sign, for Pat Toole John was in his usual post-fair condition and was lying exhausted either in the bottom of the cart or along one of the seats of the side-car. But, with *Cannon Ball* between the shafts he was in the safest possible guardianship.

So they would draw up outside Pat's cottage and *Cannon Ball* would contentedly crop the crisp grass of the verge until his lord and master woke up and turned him into his field. Pat had long been a widower, and no shrewish tongue greeted his return from market. The two went through life in perfect sympathy.

At four years, *Cannon Ball* started his stud career. Soon he was making a name for himself as a local sire; indeed as the years passed and his reputation grew there seemed to be few days on which one did not see, in the lanes leading to Pat Toole John's farm, some little mare trotting coyly to her nuptials. The Free State started a system of Government-sponsored stallions, which toured the countryside with the laudable object of improving the standard of horseflesh throughout the country. But, in our part of Connemara, the Government stallion had an empty engagement book; for the absense of the entry by *Cannon Ball* in the pedigree of a local pony put paid to its saleable value. 'By *Cannon Ball*' became a passport to fame.

The climax of *Cannon Ball*'s calendar was races day. The Oughterard races took place early in August, but for several days before that tinker's carts had groaned by our gate, and through glasses, we could spot families with their boots slung round their necks descending the mountainside across the lake opposite the lodge en route for the event of the year. From Roundstone and Recess they came,

Garnet aged 90 at Cleggan in 2003

from a score of villages hugging the wild Atlantic coast to the west of us. From the more "civilised" east came bookies from Dublin and Galway, three-card tricksters and purveyors of jellied eels. A surprising number of Cockneys were among them bent on transferring a year's savings from our rustics' unsophisticated pockets to their own.

The day began early, with much drinking of porter in the village street and a preliminary canter at spotting the lady, pea and thimble, and crown and anchor. The first official event was the bicycle race, down the road from Oughterard to Ross, three miles away, and back. It was timed for noon and was a real test for both machine and rider; for in those days the road lacked macadam and the pot-holes were formidable and deep. It was a handicap event, and the handicaps were determined primarily by the type of machine produced by the individual entrants. First away might be a middle-aged villager, clad in orthodox race-going rig of bowler hat and homespun, and riding a vintage ladies model. The back-marker, departing at least two pints later, was probably a near professional, black cycling outfit, low handlebars and all. He nearly always won — his prize £1-for the others had only entered 'for a bit of sport, Sorr'.

Bicycle race over, the whole concourse, side-shows and all, would wend their way to the race-course proper. This consisted of four fields behind the village, gaps knocked in the stone walls to let the runners through. The course was situated on a sharp slope and two sides were, in consequence, set at an alarming gradient. The card comprised four events: a donkey race, to break the ice (it nearly always succeeded in breaking up one or two stalls as well); the farmers' race; the strangers' race; and the consolation race, for 'all beaten horses'. The stakes were £3, £5, £10 and £5 respectively.

The strangers' race was well named; for an element of surprise surrounded the event and it often contained a dark horse or two. A young thoroughbred might, for example, be run for track experience, before being entered under rules, or the field might contain a horse whose owner was temporarily in the doldrums, having been warned off the more respectable forms of turf. I recall one mystery entry, whose jockey wore real colours, an unprecedented phenomenon for Oughterard. The horse not only lapped the field, but bolted and was stopped only on the outskirts of Ross, the neighbouring village.

The farmers' race was *Cannon Ball*'s very own. *Brown Jack*'s feats at Ascot fade into insignificance alongside *Cannon Ball*'s at Oughterard. The white pony won the event sixteen years running. For the first two or three he was ridden by Pat Toole John himself. Then the temptations of the village street in the forenoon proved too strong and, at the time of going to the post, Pat was unwilling to take the ride. A succession of nephews-Pat Toole Pat and Pat Toole Jim amongst them-deputised, but I doubt if the jockey really mattered very much. It seemed impossible to handicap *Cannon Ball* out of that race. Betting was out of the question; for no sensible bookie would take a wager about *Cannon Ball* and it was not worth while backing anything else.

At the end, when *Cannon Ball* was approaching twenty, it may be suspected, a fate worse than death awaited the rider of any other horse who so much as contemplated winning the race. Wisely, however, Pat Toole John took *Cannon Ball* out of the farmers' race while he was still full of running. The shame of second place or also ran was never his, when he retired from the race-course in his twenty-first year, he was still an undisputed champion. We saw them returning from Oughterard on that last night of triumph. The routine was as always: *Cannon Ball* was trotting unconcernedly down the road: Pat Toole John was lying in the bottom of the cart, if possible rather more exhausted than usual.

Cannon Ball worked on the farm, went to market and attended to his stud duties for four years more. Then he died, but it was not the rather repulsive, sordid death of old age, for old age was not a state you associated with *Cannon Ball*. He simply went to sleep one night after a normal day's work and did not wake again.

Pat Toole John was heart-broken: he was also worried. Normally there was money to be made from dead ponies. It was even worth while transporting them for flesh to the kennels of the Blazers twenty-five miles away. But such could not be the fate of *Cannon Ball*, friend and partner of twenty-four years' standing. An idea struck him, nothing less than a wake was good enough for *Cannon Ball*.

A wake it was and one of the best that had ever been held in the neighbourhood. We were invited and went. *Cannon Ball* had been moved into the yard in front of the cottage door. Dimly illuminated by oil-lamps and the thin light of the moon, he lay, still in his prime it seemed, like a pony peacefully sleeping. To some the scene might have appeared indecent — to some, profane. It did not strike us so; for this was a simple act of respect by simple people to a faithful friend. Besides, who has any right to believe that there is not a Valhalla to which good ponies go?

In the cottage, filled to overflowing, we drank much porter, we sang and, as morning came, we danced. It was dawn when we moved *Cannon Ball* back to a corner of his old field and laid him decently to rest. He had earned his retirement and he went, I know, to green pastures.

Submitted by
Miss Garnet Irwin
(1972)

Michael Tully, aged 6 with grandfather Thomas Corcoran in 1925.

Michael Tully
- Jockey and Galway Hurdle Winner 1946

Our Galway Boy

Born in 1919 to an Eyre Square Galway family with no equestrian connections, Michael Tully is chiefly remembered by an older generation of Galwegians as a local hero. Everyone in town knew the jockey who won the 1946 Galway Hurdle, aboard his own horse, beating the fancied favourite by a head to the rapturous applause of his home-town supporters. *Fair Pearl* was a gelding son of *Fair Haven*, and was schooled, work-ridden and raced by his owner. His racing colours on Hurdle Day were a Corinthians rugby jersey lent to him by Josie Owens, who was in later life to become a Mayor of Galway.

Michael sits back in his chair in his Galway living room, his individuality at eighty- four years of age still undimmed, and savours once again that great winning occasion. It was said at the time that the shout that went up as he passed the finishing post could be heard out on Galway Bay. The win was hugely popular at the time with Ballybrit punters, as Michael had told everyone in Galway he was going to win and the whole town placed bets accordingly. According to the Connacht Tribune of August 3rd of that year 'It was the most popular victory ever and great credit is due to our Galway boy for bringing off such a grand win against such terrific odds'.

Sadly, success was short-lived. This particular win is not recorded in the Ballybrit records. The Hurdle win should have netted almost five hundred pounds for the owner / jockey, but the sorry story is that a board meeting of the Racecourse Committee, approximately two weeks later, took the winner's title from him. Michael, 'busy selling horses like hot dogs in England with Frenchie Nicholson and having a great time', had forgotten an unpaid entry fee of three pounds and this was the cause of his post-race disqualification. He had tried to pay this, but too late for the authorities concerned. However, The Connacht Tribune concluded that 'he will retain the honour and glory attached to one of the finest sporting achievements in the records of the Irish Turf'.

Meanwhile, Michael was booked to ride a horse for some Galway owners at Tuam Races the day after the Hurdle. According to an old friend of his, this horse was not expected to win, but Mick knew better. The horse in question was, in fact, to be 'pulled', ie. not allowed by his jockey to win in order that the connections could have a punt another day with more attractive odds. On the strength of his much-lauded Galway Hurdle win, his friend says, 'Mickey, always the gambler, got five hundred pounds on loan from his Bank manager, put the lot on his own ride to win, and ran away with a small fortune. Naturally unwilling to face the owners and friends, who had not placed bets, he made a quick exit from the Tuam track, helped by a friend waiting with a car, and did not show his face again in Galway for forty years'.

Galway Family

Michael was not the first of his family to play the betting game. His father, Mark Tully, who had gambled the family into penury, was evicted from the publican's business and had to leave the pub he ran' at the Corner House at Eyre Square, where the Vodafone shop is today, and later, from the shop they ran in Mainguard Street. When Michael was four or five years old he suffered a cruel blow when his father finally left his wife and young family and set sail for America, never to return to Ireland.

Mark and Annie Tully, Michael's parents, about 1909.

Mark Tully in the United States, having left Ireland about 1923.

Annie, his mother, still fondly referred to as Mama by her son, overcame the difficulty of being a deserted wife in a close-knit community where everybody knew their neighbours business. Today, in the high-ceilinged living room of one of the houses she built in Galway, Michael, surrounded by memorabilia of his past life, likes to keep up to date with all aspects of racing, A lightly built figure, his flowing white beard and long hair give him a patriarchal appearance as he sits among the Racing Posts and Goff's Sales Catalogues surrounding him.

Academic Forebears

Annie was one of ten children of the Corcoran family of Castlegar on the north-eastern fringes of Galway town, and her father taught in the local Briar Hill school. As Michael tells it, his great-grandfather, Thomas Corcoran, was a Professor of Classics in St Jarlath's College in Tuam. When the Professor's small salary at the time was not sufficient to maintain his own family, the Lord Oranmore and Browne, recognising the master's proficiency in European languages, set him up in a school or Tutorial House near Claremorris, Co Mayo, where he taught French and German to the children of the landed gentry. A clever man himself though never a scholar, Michael is proud of the achievements of some notable forebears. Among these were the 19th century Galway astronomer, John Birmingham of Millbrook near Tuam; Valentine Bodkin, the last Catholic Warden of St. Nicholas Collegiate Church; while another was the First Primate of All Ireland, Anthony Blake of Irishtown. The one hazy family link to racing, a grand-uncle who wound up as a trainer in Australia, was not kindly spoken of by the family.

With a strong tradition of learning in the family it might have seemed inevitable that the young Michael would follow a solid career path, going through the educational system in true middle-class fashion and perhaps ending up as a teacher, or a doctor like his sister Eveleen. But this was not to be. His abiding wish to be with horses was, in fact, to dominate the rest of his life.

Mrs Tully and her five children, Marcus, Eveleen, Mary, Michael and Bernard, set up house in South Terrace near the Claddagh. Missing a father, the family remained close to their extended family living in and around Galway. Michael's aunt Nora Tully lived in Shop Street, another aunt ran the G.B.C Restaurant, and his mother's brother, a Canon Corcoran, ministered in Kilcreest in east County Galway, and also ran a small farm there.

Childhood country holidays

The children spent holidays with their uncle Canon Corcoran who raised Galway sheep and to the joy of two small city boys, had a pony called *Sam*. Michael remembers being too young to ride *Sam*. However, the older Marcus used to pull his younger brother up on the saddle in front of him, and in this way, they would ride and jump the pony around the farm as a twosome.

The Galway breed of sheep on the farm was a great animal for a small boy to ride as the thick fleece made falling off nearly impossible. One ram however, nearly caused a serious accident when, with small boy on board, he raced towards a 'pookhaun' (a hole in the wall specially constructed to allow lambs, but not fully grown sheep, to run through). With young Michael hanging on to the fleece, the ram charged straight for the low 'pookhaun' and was only edged aside at the last moment by the barking of their clever terrier Jeff. Sadly Michael's much-admired older brother, Marcus was to die of a perforated appendix, at the age of fifteen, in 1925.

A schoolboy in Galway, right with brother Bernard and sister Mary.

Michael, riding Galway businessman Joe Young's hunter in 1933.

Early years, Pony Racing

On holidays with his uncle, Canon Corcoran, the young Michael became involved in riding the small ponies bred by the Donohues of Woodville and by the time he was thirteen, his mother had bought his first pony and he had tried his hand at pony-racing. This pony, whose dam was Connemara, was by a Thoroughbred stallion, *Varsity Blue*. In Mama's view, nothing but the best was good enough for her favourite son and according to himself she had thoroughly spoiled him, forking out money for his every whim. With his mother's help he paid the goodly sum of eighteen pounds for his pony and off they went on the flapper racing circuit, winning at the Claddagh Races, Oughterard, Roundstone, Clifden and Gort. He often travelled with a Tom Deane of Frenchpark, Roscommon, who drove a lorry load of ponies to races all over the Western region. Michael rode some winners for him and for other owners, including Charles St. George of Tyrone House near Kilcolgan, and for many others who needed a competent rider. With his gift for remembering names he tells of two ponies which won for him at the Claddagh; they were Colie Costello's *Menlo Boy* and Tom Clancy's *Sweet Peggy*. He did not confine himself to pony racing and had his first horse winner at a Longford flapper on *Goosey Gander* at the age of sixteen.

Schooldays and Apprenticeship

After a brief and unhappy spell at Garbally College as a boarder, his mother finally gave in to his horse-centred interests and sent him off as a fee paying apprentice, as was the custom at that time, to the stable-yard of trainer Gus Mangan in Castlebaggett, now Baldonnell, Co Dublin. What afterwards became an aerodrome was at that time the Mangan gallops. It was here that he rode his first 'real race-horse' under rules. This was *Corrib Lady* owned by J.T. Costello, proprietor of the Royal Hotel in Galway. He also spent time as an assistant trainer with Darby Rogers on the Curragh,

the father of Tim and Mick Rodgers, trainers of Epsom Derby winners *Santa Claus* and *Hard Ridden*. While working for another trainer, Jack Ruttle, one of the horses he schooled was *Workman*, later to make his name as a winner of the Aintree Grand National. Other trainers he spent time with included J.J. Parkinson, Damian Malone, Jack Mahony, Tommy Jennings of Enniscorthy, and Tim Sullivan of Portmarnock
.

In the mid nineteen twenties, his mother had been lucky enough to inherit a substantial sum from a rich American uncle, George Corcoran who had made his fortune, first mining and later ranching near Santa Fe. She very sensibly decided to put this windfall into building property in Galway,both at Newcastle and on St.Mary's Road. His doctor sister, Eveleen, later lived and carried out her medical practice in one of the bigger houses on St. Mary's Road.

On Galway Hurdle Day, Michael, doing things in style, arranged to have a coach, drawn by two coloured horses, outside the house, to drive his sisters and some friends the three miles to the Ballybrit racetrack. It was also to his sister's house that the beloved *Fair Pearl*, Michael's Galway Hurdle winner in 1946, was 'honoured' by being brought up the steep steps to the spacious front hallway, at some stage during the wee hours of the night of the post-race celebrations. Eveleen would have been horrified by such frivolity but the escapade was kept from her ears!

Dealing Days and the 'blocker' Daly

A former commanding officer of the Army Equitation School, Col Liam Hayes, who was also a racing man, encouraged Michael to join the Army and with hopes of jumping for the Army Equitation School, he joined up in the late nineteen thirties. He spent a number of months at McKee Barracks, in the era of famous Irish show-jumping rider Jed

Michael is first past the post in the Independent Hurdle at Naas with **Fair Pearl**.

O'Dwyer, but never really took to show-jumping which in his view 'was not a nice game - horses don't jump of their own accord, you know'. This view may have been influenced by his own Steeple-chasing experience. Altogether, four horses ridden by him in Point to Point races fell and had to be put down and he himself also suffered injuries in these falls
.

Having met Atty Persse, owner/trainer of the famous champion two year old *The Tetrarch*, in England, he decided to use this contact to set up, in the early forties, Galway's first riding establishment at a former Persse house opposite Ardmore in Taylor's Hill, where the pitch-and-putt golf course is now. Buying horses for the riding school, he travelled to fairs, and entered the world of dealing, haggling, buying and selling. Ned Cash, one of the best-known Irish horse dealers, was a prominent buyer at the time. Michael was dealing not only in horses and ponies, but also traps, coaches and broughams and all sorts of horse drawn conveyances which he found at Fairs in Eyre Square. From Taylors Hill he rented out ponies and traps during the war years when petrol was rationed.

He was moving in a world of wheeling and dealing, meeting all sorts, the best and the worst, learning the tricks of the trade and making contacts his own middle-class family would have deemed slightly less than suitable.

He fondly recalls a pinto pony he bought for the riding school from one of the Dodds, a traveller family in Galway, and from 'Doddsie' he learned a lot and picked up some useful ways of handling horses.

From time to time he worked with one of the best-known characters frequenting Fairs at the time. This man, who was known as the 'blocker' Daly, was so called because early on Fair Day he would drive his car up to *twenty* miles away to spot horses being travelled on the country roads, before they got to the Fair. Those 'the blocker' liked, he 'raddled', meaning he marked the coat of the favoured horse lightly at the shoulder with a scissors, to make things easy for his buyer, who would then walk through the Fair checking horse shoulders and speedily choosing his purchases. The buyer they worked for, George 'Speed' Mullan, who specialised in trotters, was a good payer, and this raddling business brought in a few much needed extra pounds notes.

Exporting horses on the hoof

Many of these horses were being bought for the meat trade and Michael later got into this racket full time, when he lived at Hazelhatch *near* Dublin. Jobs were scarce and money even scarcer and for five years he worked in the business which exported up to eight hundred horses per month to Antwerp, for meat all over Europe. At the North Wall the manes and tails were stripped off these unfortunate animals and this horse-hair was sold for mattresses, fetching two shillings and ten pence a pound. Horses who died on the journey were unceremoniously thrown overboard.

He talks of a Thoroughbred mare he saved from this cruel end. He spotted her being driven up the ship's ramp with the other unfortunates and retrieved her just in time as she looked 'too good to give lead to' ie. too good for the butcher's bullet. This high-class in-foal mare was *Miss Raleigh*, who, it transpired, had been bred at Kildangan stud, and had belonged to one of the owners of the ill-fated Titanic. The mare had been trained by Joe Osborne and was dam of a race winner *No Comment*. From these heights to the hell of the slaughter boat!

Mick Tully on Fair Pearl gets up on the line to beat King of the Jungle (Danny Morgan) in a thrilling finish to the 1946 Galway Hurdle.

Fair Pearl and Dorothy Paget's **King of the Jungle** race for the finish in the Galway Hurdle in 1946.

Fair Pearl being led in by Trainer C.B. Harty after the win at Naas.

Fair Pearl

During his dealing days Michael, who periodically travelled Ireland with Frenchie Nicholson, buying up Thoroughbreds 'like hot cakes'and transporting them to England where they were sold on for a handsome profit, managed to find one horse in particular that caught his eye. As might be expected, a story comes with the purchase of Galway Hurdle hero *Fair Pearl*.

Michael, then in his mid- twenties, bought the horse one day for around two hundred pounds at Limerick. Later that same day he suffered a severe fall in a steeplehase at Limerick Junction, which left him unconscious for thirteen days. Somebody put the horse on the horse-train to Dublin where he spent three or four days at Inchicore, now Heuston station, before trainer Cyril Harty, having heard about the stranded horse, came and brought him back to his Chapelizod yard. Michael finally regained consciousness at the hospital in Tipperary where he had been brought by 'a bread van doing duty as an ambulance' after his fall, and made his way to Chapelizod to find his horse in training there with Cyril Harty. When both horse and jockey had recovered sufficiently from the Limerick experience, they went racing at Naas where the pair had their first win, the Independent Hurdle, the second biggest hurdle race in the country after Galway. This was followed by another win at Navan and he then decided to aim the horse for home and the Galway Races.

Racehorse in the suburbs

In Galway in the mid nineteen forties, Michael kept his *Fair Pearl* in a stable on Raleigh Row, a laneway just around the corner from his home on St. Mary's Rd. He loved this horse he called 'the one and only'. When the animal was unsettled in his stable and developed into a weaver, the term for a horse who stands at the stable door swaying over and back continuously, he bought a companion for

him, a goat he called Billy the Kid, for seventeen shillings and six pence. With his new friend, the horse gave up the weaving and became so attached to his stable mate that the goat also travelled to race meetings with the horse in the trailer. His owner was frequently seen riding *Fair Pearl* through the Galway streets on his way to the old racecourse at Carnmore, a few miles outside the town, to school and gallop him there. However, the Salthill beaches were his principal training ground and he is remembered by older townspeople for his gallops along the large expanse of the Grattan Road beach for three weeks before the Hurdle.

A move to England

After the big *Galway Hurdle* win and, as he himself admits 'with more money than sense' he decided to bring Fair Pearl to England. There he was placed in races at Manchester, Cheltenham and Worchester but never carried off a win. His best performance was in the Queen Mother's Champion Chase where he came third and he managed a fourth in the four mile National Hunt Chase in Cheltenham.

Michael's jockey friend Frenchie Nicholson, who was later to run a renowned riding academy at Cheltenham, was then starting to train horses and had wanted to buy the horse. Nevertheless, his owner, broke at the time, sold, or as he says himself, pawned *Fair Pearl* to a Mrs. Hopley who lived in the Abbeyville Estate in North Co. Dublin, for two thousand, five hundred pounds. Some time later when he sought to retrieve the pawned horse, his new owner refused to let him go as he had come second and third for her and she expected him to move into the top place fairly soon. *Fair Pearl*, however, never won for Mrs.Hopley. Michael claims that those minding him did not give him the special treatment to which he had become accustomed, such as getting him to lie down at night to rest completely, using an *old* method he

*Michael on a rare visit to Galway in July 1987, with **Clogs**, owned by Dominick St. owner-trainer John Monroe.*

*With old friend **Teleprompter** in Richmond, England.*

himself had learned from his traveller friend 'Doddsie'.

The 'big job' and moving on

Michael had reluctantly pawned Fair Pearl because he needed the money for the 'big job' in England with Major Powell near Lambourn. With the revival of Racing after the War in England, there was a general exodus of Irish jump jockeys to try their luck across the Irish Sea. There he became a professional jockey and helped run a racing yard with seventy eight horses. He moved on to work with Paul Davey at Norton up in Yorkshire and some time later moved back to Newmarket to an eighty-eight horse-yard which included sixty two-year-olds racehorses, the majority of which had to be ridden out each morning by a couple of stable lads and himself.

Later he worked with Joe Mercer, a flat racing jockey who was to ride over two thousand winners before he retired in 1985, in a yard which kept one thousand Thoroughbreds, near Newbury in Berkshire.

In his years in England he experienced working with a variety of trainers, moving on regularly, because as he says himself, he 'wasn't a yes man'. He had learned the hard truth that in those times, the late forties and early fifties, *'jockeys were, like other professional sportsmen, neither paid very well nor respected very much by the class of person who employed them'*
(Eamon Dunphy, Sunday Independent, Oct 25,1987).

He spent time working as head lad for Michael Beary, a top Irish jockey in England and also for Tom Yates and for another successful jockey 'Cock of the North' Billy Nevett who trained near Ripon. By 1951 he was deputy head-man with Major F.B Sneyd at Sparshalt, a vet who had unique training ideas which he enjoyed discussing with Michael.

He remembers him as 'the cleverest trainer I ever worked with'.

Fred Winter

Ryan Price, one of those he helped to get started as a trainer, became a highly successful jumps trainer between 1945 and 1970, and was Champion Trainer five times *Michael* recalls a day in Ryan Price's yard where a quiet stable lad was sweeping up. This quiet lad was later to be hailed as the greatest of all steeplechase jockeys, Fred Winter. In partnership with trainer Ryan Price, Winter excelled, winning the Champion Jockey title four times. He is probably best remembered for his incredible feat of winning the Grand Steeplechase de Paris without a bit in the horse's mouth, when the bit had broken after three fences.

Michael, some years later, was to make the acquaintance of Fred Winter's mother, when, one Sunday morning he drove past her on the road, stopped to offer her a lift, to which she responded in a broad Dublin accent that it was to 'bloody Mass' she was walking. She was, it transpired, a Flanagan from Dublin's Coombe area and after that they were to become good friends and he often drove her to Mass in Newmarket church on Sunday mornings.

He regularly saw Lester Piggott riding out as a young lad near Lambourn. The young Lester, it was not generally known, had a hearing and speech impediment, but the impression given was that he was so well minded by his parents that he was not allowed to speak to the perceived riff raff of the horsey world i.e the stable lads and jockeys he rode out with.

Horses galore and empty pockets

In 1959 Michael went to work as Head Lad at Sam Hall's Brecongil stables at the north of England racing centre, Middleham, in North East Yorkshire.

*Tracey Piggott interviews Michael at Ballybrit racecourse in 2000,
holding a copy of that week's Connacht Tribune which re-tells the
story of the Galway Hurdle win.*

Michael in retirement but still immersed in the racing world.

On arrival he was given fifty-odd horses and instructed to 'do what you like with them'. In the event the horses did some winning and Michael was to work for Sam Hall, off and on, for some ten years. After a disagreement with the trainer he left but when Sam's niece, Sally, inherited Brecongil after Sam's departure to another yard in 1969, she re-hired him and he travelled back to Middleham again.

Michael himself notched up thirty or forty professional rides in a racing career which spanned the 1930's, 40's and 50's. He was placed eight or ten times including a third in the Stayers Hurdle at Cheltenham, when riding for Major Powell. It was a time when he became familiar with the crooked as well as the straight edge of the sport, when, he admits, race-rigging was commonplace. Stable lads were paid a pittance and to keep money in his pocket he spent long periods working in a car factory at Cowley assembling Hillman Huskies, and occasionally joined the pick-and-shovel brigade along with other Irish labourers, but he always returned to work with horses when opportunities arose.

Throughout his life, despite all the difficulties and setbacks he experienced, his chief ambition was to stay involved in the world of horse-racing. He cared for his horses in a manner both personal and professional and was always kind to them. Because he liked them, was known to have a special way with them and to have a good influence on his charges, he was often sent to accompany horses, in the early days of transporting them long distances by plane. He became familiar with far-flung racecourses at Hong Kong, Malaya, Bombay in India and Pakistan. Kuala Lumpur was memorable as he was stuck for weeks because of the Civil War in Sri Lanka.in 1983. He recalls experiencing turbulence while travelling fifty-eight horses to Sydney in a huge transport Flying Tiger plane and trying to keep the horses calm. He was also given the job of transporting police guard dogs in crates by plane to Johannesburg during the days of South Africa's apartheid regime.

Return to Ballybrit Racecourse

In the millennium year of 2000 Michael Tully made his first appearance at Ballybrit racecourse since his victory of fifty-four years previously. It was the occasion when he was invited to the Parade Ring to be interviewed for RTE by Tracey Piggott. Many years previously he had worked for her grandfather Fred Armstrong in England and he was delighted to recount the details of his famous Hurdle win with *Fair Pearl* and to re-live some of the glory and the excitement of a never-to-be-forgotten race. Many old Galway people, watching him on TV, remembered that day too and recalled him riding through the narrow Galway streets on Fair Pearl or galloping along the beach below Grattan Road, and some remembered the goat who often accompanied horse and rider in such very different times.

After a period spent travelling the world he finally returned to retire and settle back to life in Galway, closely following the Thoroughbred and racing scene and 'talking horses' whenever the opportunity arose. The names come tripping off the tongue of the 84 year old, he remembers all of them, with a smile for one, a scowl for another; the trainers, owners jockeys, some stable lads who made it as champion jockey, their good and their bad points. The work was tough for all involved, on a seven day a week basis, living conditions often primitive and he himself regularly schooled from eight to twelve horses a day. He knew the seed, breed and generation of the horses and of the people who worked with them. Rolling stone that he was, they are as clear in his mind as though it all happened yesterday.

Chapter 3

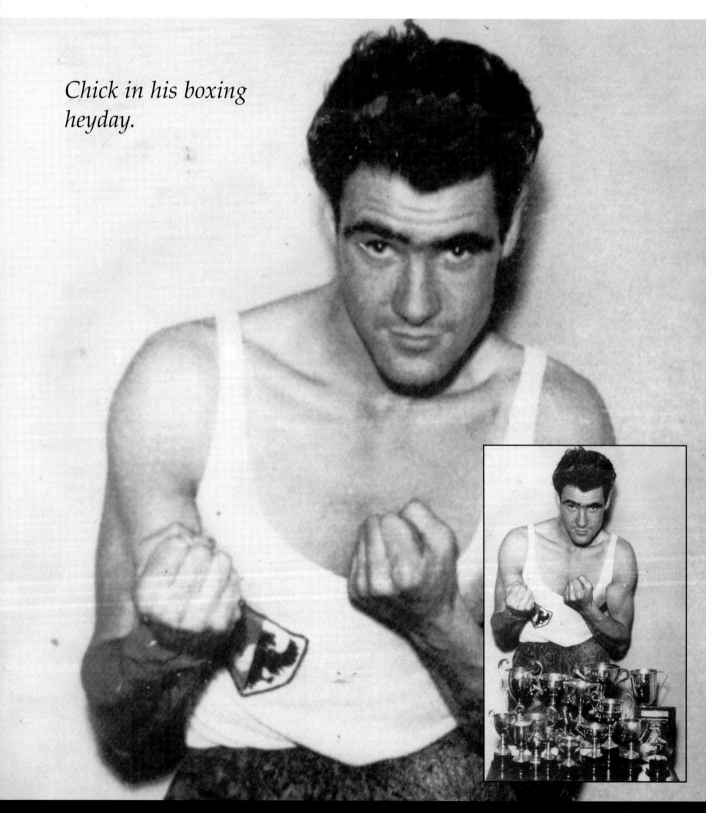

Chick in his boxing heyday.

Chick Gillen
Boxer, City Barber and Country Sportsman

begann his lifelong interest in matters equine when, as a boy, he helped Mary Long of Rosshill, on the east side of Galway, to deliver milk door to door with her pony and cart. His payment was to hop up and have a ride on the pony when the milk deliveries were done.

Michael Gillen or 'Chick' as he is best known, was always prominent in boxing circles in Galway having been Connacht and Army Champion a number of times as well as boxing successfully at National level. Down through the years he freely gave of his time and energy, his boxing skills and above all his encouragement to Galway's young aspiring boxers. He gave time especially to the boys from the Traveller community who tended to be left on the margins of society to fend for themselves. A Boxing Club coach and mentor, he paved the way for the career of the young Francis Barrett, who went on to qualify for the 2000 Olympics and who subsequently carried the flag for Ireland in the Atlanta Stadium parade. The boxer was interviewed by the media on the TV screens for days afterwards, each time thanking Chick as the foremost influence on his life by providing the boxing premises and equipment in Galway and for making it possible for him to train in his sport and participate in the Olympics. Francis Barrett is currently reigning European light welter-weight Champion and is still in regular touch with his mentor in Galway.

Already known in Galway by the many to whom the helping hand had been extended, Chick became renowned throughout the rest of the country after the Olympics.

Bohermore Boxer

What wasn't well-known was that the same level of altruism also extended into the world of 'our four-legged friends', and Chick had always owned a few horses and ponies, since he paid £100 for his first horse, Big Tom, at the last Fair in Galway which was held in the Fair Green. He regularly gave youngsters from his own area of Mervue the opportunity to jump his ponies at local Gymkhanas and to ride them in Pony Racing events.

Although he has lived in Mervue since 1957, he was born and reared in Bohermore, where his uncle and grandfather were carters, where he well remembers his biggest thrill as a boy was to get a spin on the carter's horse. After the horse's working day local kids were allowed hop up for a spin to ride the animal back to the fields in Terryland, where gymnastics and cossack-like riding tricks were practised on the cart-ponies before letting them get to their well-earned grass. In Bohermore too, he learned his boxing skills, sparring with other local lads, under a street lamp at night, in Cooke's Terrace, outside the house of a friendly old lady, and there too he picked up the nickname 'chick' from a well-known character, 'the game chicken', in the comics of those times.

The 'Flapps'

Married to Maureen from Dublin- whose father had worked a dairy pony in the capital — they gave their five children every opportunity to learn to ride and to care for the family's ponies. They also fostered two boys 'who were just like family' with their own children.

Stalwart Bohermore boxers in 1949.

Back: Eamon Fitzpatrick, John Harlowe, Chick Gillen, Mattie Maloney.

Front: Georgie Peters, Sean Thornton, Sailor Folan, Sean Bohan.

As the children grew up, they rode and hunted and went Pony Racing or Flapping, as it was known. This was an informal type of racing which catered for every type of equine — except the regal Thoroughbred — and has always been a popular local event in the Irish countryside. Races were held for three heights of ponies and also for horses. Some of the latter were indeed Thoroughbreds on a quiet practice-run for the real Races, ie. racing under Turf Club Rules. A carthorse race, a farmer's race and a donkey derby were usually included in the day's programme, as were bicycle races and children's Sports.

'Flapps' were held in, among other places, Tuam, Dunmore, Oughterard and Clifden in Co.Galway, on various strands in Connemara and in parts of Co. Clare and in Kerry. According to Chick, Dingle in Co. Kerry was the Curragh of Flapping in Ireland, where the track has its own stand and pony-owners convened from all parts of Ireland and from England, to try their luck. The Dingle Derby was known to be the most important pony-race in the country. However, in the eyes of the Irish Turf Club it was the most prominent, and highly illegal, flapper fixture in the country, notorious as a venue for shady racing practices. It was not unknown for racehorses to run under false names at Dingle and it was strictly out of bounds to the racing fraternity and jockeys were not even allowed to attend, even as spectators.

Claddagh Races Revival

There had been Pony Racing in the 'Swamp'in the Claddagh area of Galway in the 1930's and again in 1956 and 1957 when the Dominick Street and William Street West Traders Association had sponsored a revival. Small fields at both these meetings were probably the reason why the Sponsors, in 1958, moved their money to Terrier Racing in Pearse Stadium in Salthill. Chick, however, always kept a few donkeys for. Donkey

Derbies which were held in Salthill, as well as some cross-bred hunting dogs known as 'lurchers', for field- coursing in winter-time

Bringing his own family round the Racing circuit he got the idea of bringing Pony Racing back to the Claddagh. Early in 1971 Chick and some other racing fans came together in Galway's Atlanta Hotel and decided they were going to equal the popularity of Dingle's good points by organising a revival of the old tradition of Pony Racing in Galway. The large area of windswept open land between the Claddagh and the sea, variously known as the Swamp and more recently, South Park, would again be the venue, after a lapse of some fifteen years, for all of the high jinks and entertainment that went along with the Pony Racing.

This small group formed an ad-hoc committee and secured the sponsorship of the same Dominick St. and William St. West Traders Association who had supported the Racing in the mid-fifties. In the months that followed they put an enormous amount of work into getting their project off the ground and it was decided to run the Pony Racing in conjunction with the newly proposed Claddagh Festival. The old thatched village, the oldest part of Galway, once said to have been the largest fishing village in Ireland, had been replaced in the 1930's with "more sanitary habitations". While better housing was definitely needed for the inhabitants, it was said that the old community spirit of the place had been adversely affected with the dissolution of the old village. The purpose of the Festival was not only to raise money for a new Community Centre but to 'preserve and strengthen the traditional spirit of neighbourliness among the people and give them a greater community pride' (Connacht Tribune).

Claddagh Races mid-seventies.

Claddagh Festival Programme of Events

A very 'full, varied and attractive' eight-day programme was launched, beginning with the installation of the veteran fisherman, Martin Oliver, who, as King of the Claddagh, was to arrive in a brown-sailed hooker to be presented with a fish, the traditional symbol of office in this fishing village, and the King was also to officiate at an open-air concert. 'On opening day the pier was crowded with dignitaries as the Mayor, Councillor Michael Smyth, in scarlet robe, was escorted in by the bearers of the city's ancient sword and mace and he was accompanied by robed members of the Borough Council'.The day was pronounced 'a huge success' and for a week in August for the following seven years, something of the old Claddagh spirit of friendliness and co-operation was revived and fostered.

In this era of carnivals, festivals, dance halls and dance bands, the Festival Marquee hosted top flight bands every night for a week, with heats each night for the title of Claddagh Princess and the Festival's Grand Finale would be the selection of the Festival Princess at the final night's Big Dance. The biggest single event was to be the Claddagh Races on the Bank Holiday Monday, and with over 100 entries from all four provinces and eight races planned, including a Donkey Derby and Carthorse Race, it was all set for success.

In the course of the week all sorts of activities took place. There was a Yachting Regatta, Giant Bingo, Concerts by St Mary's Housewives Club, Sports, Art competition, Childrens Fancy Dress, Baby show, Puc Fada, Cic Fada, Tug O'War, Displays of baking, with linen and crochet. There was also Ladies Soccer (Single Rovers v. Married United. sic!), A Walter Macken play, 'Home is the Hero', Five a-side Socccr, Billiards and Snooker and Table-Tennis competitions, a Feis, Sea Angling and Clay Pigeon Shooting. It was billed to be, not only the best Festival in the West, but in the whole country. Large numbers of local people became involved, as the organisational requirements were prodigious.

Pony Racing, the Main Annual Event

The Claddagh Festival ran annually until 1978 and the main event, held on the August Bank Holiday Sunday or Monday, was the Pony Racing. Crowds of people came to South Park, over twenty bookies attended and betting was keen. Eight Races were normally billed with from four to eight ponies or horses going to post, mainly Connemara ponies and part-breds but with the occasional Thoroughbred. In the later seventies the initial momentum was still there and in 1977 a five-a-side soccer tournament, a ballad competition, a five-a-side Gaelic football tournament and childrens Sports were advertised. The new King of the Claddagh, Patrick 'Ladineen' Curran, presided and presented the Kings Cup to the winner of the Open Pony Race. This race was listed in the programme as the 'H.H. King Patrick Curran Royal Stakes' and Chick's daughter Linda, was to win this trophy two years running, with both *Mervue Pride* and *Galway Girl*.

Cart-Horse Race and Donkey Derby

The cart-horse race or 'The Land Gallop for Cart-Horses' as it was quaintly billed, was the specialty of the Fahy family whose horse, always ridden bareback, and known as *Pin Cushion*, won this race a couple of years running. The Feeney family were regular contenders and Tom Feeney, whose father Thomas served on the committee, won this race on *Silver Star* in the first Festival year. The Claddagh Plate and the Claddagh Hooker Stakes, were other hotly contested Races.

The day was brought to a close by the Donkey Derby, sponsored by Chick Gillen, and for some spectators the highlight of the week. Chick recalls

Colie Flaherty Mor with P.J. Ruane's last carthorse. Both horse and Colie, a know athlete, had competed in the Claddagh Races in their younger days.

Special Olympics 1996
Chick with Rory O'Toole, Swimming champion, Special Olympics, in the barber's shop

up to sixteen donkeys being involved on occasion, as well as many of the colourful and imaginative names given to some of these donkeys: The Griffin family produced *Rahoon Slasher* annually, and there was *Mervue Bus*, *Salthill Snob*, *Skinhead* and *Dirty Dick*. Also running were *Bohermore Harrier*, *Tarmacadam Lad* and *Miami Beach*. Chick himself regularly ran the less flamboyantly named *Coco*. He was a committee member and also a Race Starter for a couple of years; he always had a runner and sons Patrick Joseph and Michael were regular jockeys.

Accidents and the End of Claddagh Racing

Accidents were not unknown at The Swamp, even though the meeting was now run under the rules of the Pony Racing Association (WPRA) as it was difficult to provide adequate stewarding in such a large open area. Ponies sometimes proved unmanageable for their child riders and the restraining rope marking the course was not a very effective barrier. There is a story of a pony once leaving the track and flying down over the pebble beach, into the water where he proceeded to swim out to sea. Mercifully he had dropped his jockey first, as the pony finally swam ashore a considerable distance away. Another time when one novice pony failed to make a sharp bend, the rest followed it through the ropes, jumping car bonnets and causing mayhem, putting hoofs through windscreens and scattering the crowd.

But it was in 1978 that a serious accident occurred when a five-year old child wandered out on the track just after a race had started. Thomas Feeney, one of the race organisers, ran on to the track, throwing himself on top of the child to save her from the galloping hooves. The little girl was not too badly injured but her rescuer's gallant deed almost cost him his life. That year saw the end of the Pony Racing in the Claddagh. Soaring insurance costs now meant the day out was no longer a viable proposition.

Gymkhanas and Fund Raising events

However, Chick was not one to let things lie, and mindful of all the fun and enjoyment the ponies had given to himself and others during the Racing years, he successfully organised a Gymkhana in South Park, borrowing a set of jumps, publicising the event by informing all the pony people throughout the county, securing sponsorship and even getting St. Patrick's brass band to attend. He repeated the Gymkhana the following year, but insurance costs again ruled out the continuation of this event on an annual basis.

Undaunted, on another occasion when the Boxing Club needed the where-with-all to send a team to compete in England, he decided to run a fund-raising event in the grounds of the Holy Family School in Renmore. As ever, the day was organised around animals with dog-racing as well as ponies, and of course a donkey derby. People brought all sorts of dogs to race and they careered all over the place as, unfortunately, the electric hare had broken down. It was only when a boy ran the course, well ahead, with a dead rabbit, as in a drag hunt, that the dogs realised the name of the game and stayed with the scent, helped by their owners running with them. The running boy at some stage looked behind him, saw the dogs catching up, threw the rabbit in one direction and wisely ran in the other.

Most importantly, the event, as well as being an entertaining day out for local families, raised enough money to bring twenty six Galway boxers to Manchester. Chick thrived on organising such events, stressing that help was always forthcoming in those days when people seemed never 'too busy' to help out, and expensive insurance was not always a problem back then.

*Linda on **Sandy** in 1976 receives the King's Cup from Claddagh King 'Ladineen' Curran.*

*Chick's daughter Linda, taking part in an Amateurs show-jumping competition at the RDS with **Galway Girl** in the early seventies.*

*Michael Gillen rode **Pasha** in the Claddagh Races.*

*Patrick Joseph, aged six, on **Pasha**.*

Country Sports

Reminiscing, he enthuses about the life he's had: 'It's been a wonderful life; not drinking or smoking but instead, hunting, shooting, fishing, flapping, lamping, and coursing.' Born and bred a 'townie' he somehow managed to enthusiastically combine all these animal-linked country pursuits with his job as a popular barber in his Dominick Street premises. He also coached boxers two days a week, served as a fireman and is remembered by Seapoint dancers in the fifties as a polite uniformed bouncer at that popular dance-hall.

On three or more mornings a week in summer Chick was to be found Game shooting with a couple of pals, which involved going out to the Oranmore or Maree countryside at five a.m and being back in time for work by nine.

Lamping involved going out with a few friends and dogs on a night-time hunting expedition in Winter and was a sort of coursing exercise for the dogs, in the days before muzzles became obligatory for that pastime.

It might not be a very common country sporting activity nowadays but in earlier, less squeamish times, in the fifties, for example, lamping was widespread. A Department of Agriculture subsidy was paid for killing foxes, and the July Connacht Tribune reported in 1957 that two hundred and ninety foxes had been killed over a couple of months in Roscommon, an indication of the lucrative nature of the business of exporting fox furs. Rabbits in addition were 'a pest responsible for the widespread destruction of green crops and were alarmingly numerous' and lamping as one of the means of dealing with these pests was a common pastime back then.

Rabbits were the main prey, and dazzled by the torchlight, they were an easy quarry for the pursuing dogs and were despatched by a man with a quick blow to the back of the head. Rabbits were popular for the dinner in the 50's when rabbit soup and meat was supposed to be a preventative and also a cure for ulcers. Hares were never 'lamped' when Chick was involved as 'hares were different' and he could not bear to hear the cry of an injured hare — like the cry of a child. Fishing was yet another pastime and he still keeps a boat on the Corrib, and holds on to a couple of ponies as well.

Pony Racing or Flapping, in Chicks opinion, was always fun, informal and friendly. In recent times it has become recognised as an important training ground for jockeys of the future and many a top jockey of today started off and gained valuable experience on the Pony Racing circuit. Chick is pleased that a grandson of his is now involved in the sport and especially so now that helmets and body protectors are compulsory for all riders. More popular than ever, better stewarded and with more concerns for safety, Pony Racing as a sport of the countryside is definitely set to stay.

Chapter 4

*Jumping **Grey Dawn** to win at Oughterard Show in 1947,*

Commandant Eamon O'Donohue
Army Show-jumping
Team Rider

M cKee Barracks,

located on the appropriately named Blackhorse Avenue at the city edge of Phoenix Park, is an oasis of horse-centred activity close to the heart of the city of Dublin. Since its foundation in 1926, the Army Equitation School has brought to the old red brick buildings and spacious yards of the former barracks, a quality of dedicated horsemanship and military diligence which has produced top class Irish horses and riders for almost 80 years. Since the early 1930's — excluding the War years when all competition stopped — the army horses and riders have successfully taken on the rest of the world in both Show-jumping and, to a lesser extent, Eventing.

Eamon O'Donohue from Galway was one of these riders. He served in the Army until 1980, and lived here at McKee until he met and married a Co. Galway girl, Vera Killilea, in 1962, when he moved to live a short distance away from the Equitation School. The Army life he unequivocally describes as "wonderful, we had a great time". Courteous and soft-spoken, he is a serious and engaging character and one can easily envisage him having possessed a calm and easy way in his dealings with horses.

Childhood ponies
The highlights of his early days in late 1930's Galway, at three or four years of age, were the early morning rides on the pony and cart of Tommie Cosgrave of Bushypark who delivered milk to the house of his parents Louvaine and Eddie O'Donohue, on St. Marys Road. The childhood memory of his fondness for the cart pony stayed with him and was eventually to shape his future career with horses when, as a young man, he joined the Army Equitation School and fulfilled his highest expectations.

When his family moved back to his grandmother's house in High Street (where Kenny Books is today), in the early forties, the young boy wanted nothing more than to spend time at the nearby stable yard of his uncle, Eddie Shea who kept ponies just around the corner from High Street. There was a small square, known as The Parade, which contained some old stables, near the Spanish Arch where New Docks Road is today.

This was the uncle who in earlier years had acquired something of a reputation for trotting round by the nearby docks and exercising his ponies by jumping them over the fish boxes, leading to complaints from fishermen and harbour officials alike!

Galway Pony Riders
By age eight, Eamon was getting riding lessons from Dick Curley and his daughter Patsy, who had stables just off Eyre Square at Prospect Hill. Eamon's father bought a few ponies from Curleys including the Connemara mare *Grey Dawn*, who was to become his finest jumper, and who was to help make his boyhood years memorable. With four legs under him, he began the Sunday morning routine of hacking out from the town, with other young riders, to Ballyloughane Beach at Renmore, for Sunday morning lessons on the strand, given by Dick Curley.

Some of the pony owning families of that time included the Whelans, the Curleys, the Flemings, the Brennans, all with a number of children, who rode, travelling in convoy, to Shows close to Galway, or in winter time to hunts with Molly O'Rourke and the North Galway Hunt or with the Blazers. He describes a trek undertaken by a group

Eamon and **Grey Dawn** take the stone-wall at Galway Show in the Sportsground.

Proud parents Eddie and Louvaine O'Donohue

Eamon's first Rosette, on his Connemara pony, **Grey Dawn** at Ballindine gymkhana.in 1947.

Hunting with the Galway Blazers. Ita Brennan on right on **Bonnie**.

to a hunt near Athenry, which involved a fourteen mile hack to the meet, a day jumping the Galway stone walls and then the long ride home, dead tired, in the dark and freezing cold! He recalls that some of the girls in the group opted out of riding home, so the chivalrous boys had to take and lead another pony each. The noted stamina of the Connemara ponies they all rode was tested to the full on outings like this. He remembers the aches and pains as it took days for the young riders to recover from the stiffness and the tiredness, but undeterred they probably took on a similar punishing expedition the following week, such was their 'addiction'. This group of pony riders organised many long rides and outings at weekends such as paper chases and beach rides and thoroughly enjoyed themselves with their ponies.

Gymkhanas and Horse Shows

Although the Galway group hacked to the nearer County Galway Shows in convoy, sometimes an open lorry was rented to take six or eight ponies to a Show further afield such as Loughrea or Ballindine. These were ordinary cattle lorries without the partitions of a modern horse lorry, and it was necessary for each rider to travel in the lorry, everyone holding on to his or her own pony, as they bumped and rattled along the country roads, never thinking of the possible road-safety hazards of such a trip.

The Shows were a family day out and Eddie and Louvaine, who enjoyed these outings, were generally there as staunch supporters with the younger family members in tow. The Gymkhanas provided a fair share of fun and games, all was not serious competitive show-jumping. Musical chairs, fancy dress on ponies, and style and appearance classes all made for a relaxed and enjoyable day, for both families and competitors alike.

On one occasion at Galway Show in the Sportsgrounds, he remembers being disappointed to have four faults in the pony competition he had hoped to win, coming third. He asked his mother if he could take his pony *Grey Dawn* in the Novice Horse jumping. To this plan she agreed and giving him the entry fee of one pound she cautioned 'but don't tell your father', who would have said no, he was not ready for horse classes. In this competition he beat the well known show-jumper John Daly who was jumping a young horse called *The Quiet Man*, named after the recently made film in which the Dalys, of Lough Mask House in Mayo, featured with their horses. He was to remember this occasion about twelve years later when the Irish Olympic Team, staying at the same stables near Rome as the Italian Team, had become good friends with the Italian riders. Due to a mix-up one day, it happened that the Irish team horses were already loaded for the return journey to their Italian barracks and there was no available horse for Eamon to ride into the arena for a prize-giving ceremony. Reymundo D'Inzeo kindly offered him a mount. Imagine his surprise when the horse taken out of the stable ready for him to ride, turned out to be *The Quiet Man*, Reymondo's brilliant Irish jumper! Riding the horse round the Rome Olympic Arena was a strange feeling and brought him right back to his pony Show-jumping days in Galway.

Country life in the town

Galway beaches were a favourite riding venue, where ponies were schooled and exercised to prepare for the weekend Shows and Eamon often exercised ponies on the strand at Grattan Road beach, a short hack from the stables and his home. As a boy, like so many pony owners, he did all the yard work himself, mucking out, grooming, feeding, the tack cleaning, bringing ponies to be

*Eamon and **Garryowen** compete at the Dublin Spring Show in 1959.*

First Army contact. Eamon being presented with prize at Athenry Show 1951 by Lieutenant Colonel Lewis and Lieutenant Colonel McLoughlin from the Army Equitation School

Captain Jed O'Dwyer, a Limerick man and member of the acclaimed pre-war Army Jumping Team

Colonel Paul Rodzianko brought new riding and jumping methods to the Army Equitation School from 1928 on.

Eamon as a young Army Rider.

shod to Fintan Coogan in New Road, one of the last city farriers who practised hot shoeing in his forge complete with fire, bellews and hammering iron shoes into shape. Bedding was conveniently available in the form of bags of shavings from McDonaghs timber mill across the road. He enjoyed all the work associated with keeping ponies and loved being in their company. Urban pony owners at this time, in 1940's Galway, were still able to ride safely on the traffic-free streets and had the luxury of living a type of 'rus in urbe' existence with their ponies. They lacked only grazing and hay for their animals, and had to move outside the city boundaries to obtain these luxuries.

Saving the hay

The annual trip for hay was one of his happy summertime memories. Come the spring, a few of the pony owning fathers would, between them, purchase a hayfield somewhere on the eastern outskirts, like Castlegar. When the weather was opportune and the grass ready for cutting, a group of them would head out of town, carrying hay forks and rakes and work all day for two or three days until all the hay was cut, turned and cocked. The mothers, in time honoured fashion, carried out tea and food to the field workers during each day of haymaking. One of the Curley ponies, *Silva*, pulled a trap and in the field she was harnessed to an automatic hay rake, some six or eight foot wide, which was driven along by Eamon whenever he could get this favoured job. The haycocks had then to be transported back to the city in carts where storage space was a problem for some, although the O'Donohue yard luckily had space.

While the Shows and Gymkhanas usually took place at the weekends they were sometimes held on a weekday and this meant getting special permission to miss school. Like his own father Eddie, the other boys' dads were strict disciplinarians, and pony pals like Paul Fleming,

Joe Curly and Gay Whelan as well as Eamon had to obey the law as laid down by father. His other friends in St. Joseph's secondary school, 'the Bish', while not in the least envious, just thought them a bit odd for wanting to go off to Shows instead of taking part in the usual school sports of football and rowing.

As a young lad he harboured a determination to be a racing jockey, a plan which did not find favour in the O'Donohue household. They sent their son to talk to Galway's best known jockey, Michael Tully, who appears elsewhere in these pages. Here Eamon was presented with such a dark picture of the entire racing experience, that he returned home a totally disillusioned lad, finally in agreement with his parents that the horse racing track was not one for him to follow.

Military Horsemen and the Army Equitation School.

While his family would have liked him to apply for the Engineering course in University College, Galway, his heart was set on working with horses, and in fact his parents had a hard time getting him to concentrate on his studies for the Leaving Cert as he would much rather spend his time working with the ponies down in the yard.

As it happened, fate intervened when he managed to miss the qualifying entrance exam for the University course which was held on the same day as the Dublin interview for the Equitation School.

At western Shows he had regularly came in contact with Army riders who were much admired for their disciplined and impeccable horsemanship skills. These men were totally positive about the job they did and Captain Michael.Tubridy in particular, who jumped *Ballynonty*, was this young showjumper's particular hero. Capt. Tubridy encouraged him to apply for a cadetship with a view to being trained

*With **Ballycotton** at the White City International Horse Show in 1959.*

*At Pau in France with **Cill an Fháill***

*Competing for the Dublin Aga Khan Nations Cup trophy with **Cluain Meala** before the Rome Olympics.*

by the Army Equitation School. A summer course with Iris Kellett at her Mespil Road Riding School, confirmed him in this decision.

Another strong influence was that of Colonel Dan Corry, a Loughrea man, who was involved in the Army Equitation School for 32 years since it's foundation in 1926. With Red Hugh he was one of those early riding combinations who had been trained, along with Fred Aherne and Limerick men, Jed O'Dwyer and Cyril Harty, to take on the best in Europe in the Show-jumping arena.

Colonel Paul Rodzianko

Their instructor, a refugee from the Communist system in Russia, was a Colonel Paul Rodzianko who brought new riding and jumping methods to the Army School in 1928, including the forward jumping seat which was to universally replace the old backward-leaning hunting position in the Show-jumping arena. Col Rodzianko, who had been an Officer in the Tzar's Bodyguard, had instructed in the Russian Cavalry School at St. Petersburg, and had studied at the Italian Cavalry School under the maestro, Captain Federico Caprilli, who had evolved the forward seat to keep the rider above the horse's centre of gravity and who was one of the greatest teachers in the art of Show-jumping.

During his four years as Chief Instructor Col. Rodzianko worked his riders to the bone. Six hours in the saddle each day was not unusual. The hard work paid off when they had their first Aga Khan win in 1928, then took on 'the world'. During a ten year period the Team won 20 Nations Cups, competing throughout Europe and in the U.S. and was recognised as the most successful jumping team in the world. With the outbreak of the War in 1939 the Equitation School was shut down and the jumping horses put out to grass. After the War some of the previous competition horses came in

from grass, and in 1945 another strong team emerged but generally money was in short supply and there was difficulty acquiring the best horses, and this situation became the norm for about ten years. In fact it was not until the mid sixties that the Royal Dublin society decided to award prize money to the Aga Khan winners, and by then teams had become mixed civilian and army.

Seamus Hayes, Chief Instructor.

Col. Rodzianko had returned to the Equitation School to instruct again in 1950-'51, to be followed in the mid-fifties by Seamus Hayes. Having been leading show-jumper for a number of years in Britain, he was appointed Chief Instructor and for a three year term he brought a practical, rather than theoretical approach to the job. According to Eamon 'he could do anything, and demonstrated everything'. During one lesson he placed a small cigarette pack at a certain spot in front of the fence, claiming the horse would take off directly from the cigarette pack, which he did, perfectly as usual. When the Instructor's back was turned one of the students moved the package nearer the fence. Coming up to the jump, Seamus Hayes bellowed 'who moved the bloody cigarette pack? He took off from the pack at very close quarters and again executed a perfect jump.

He left soon afterwards to get back to his show-jumping life of competition, which he had to forgo during his time as an Army Instructor. He is mainly remembered for his partnership with the great horse *Goodbye*, winner of two Hickstead Derbies and later in the 60's winning countless major competitions. Other Instructors from that period were Fred Aherne, Dan Corry, Jed O'Dwyer and Jim Neylon.

By the mid fifties, when Eamon arrived on the scene, military riding had decreased although many countries, such as Italy, France, Russia,

Irish Press Cartoon depicting the teams involved in the 1960 Aga Khan competition

The opening ceremony at the Rome Olympic Stadium 1960.

*2nd in the Nations' Cup win at Nice 1960. Eamon on **Loch and Easpaig**, Bill Ringrose, **Ballynonty**, Eddie Maloney, **Glenamaddy** and Sean Daly.*

Switzerland, Argentina, Mexico and Great Britain still maintained a military interest. Increasingly civilian riders were appearing on the scene, although it was not until 1963 that professional civilian riders were to come on board the Irish Team.

Team selection and a new Career

Eamonn and his friend Ned Campion had been the pair selected by the Equitation School to train for the show-jumping team, the only two from a class of twenty hopefuls.

Four years after joining the Army, and having served as a cadet based in the Curragh for two years, Eamon jumped *Garryowen* at the 1959 Dublin Spring Show. He made his international debut riding *Ballycotton* at London's White City in August of that year, competing against top English riders such as Harvey Smith and David Broome. Iris Kellett, his former teacher, also represented Ireland there, riding *Rusty* to win the Queen Elizabeth Cup.

Over the next six years, as Lieutenant Eamon O'Donohue he was to travel to France, Italy, Spain, Belgium, Holland, Switzerland the U.S and Canada. Captain William Ringrose, Captain Roger Moloney, and Lieutenants Pat Griffin and Sean Daly among others, were his travelling companions. Army discipline, although strict, he never found a problem as 'life for children in the forties, in both the home and at school, in pre-television days, had always been disciplined'.

Olympic Games in Rome

The Rome Olympics in 1960 was his first major European foray. It was a long way from a young lad's first rosette in the Musical Chairs in Ballindine in 1947 and was certainly a memorable event, although coming perhaps a little early for the team involved. He recalls spectating at the formal opening of the Games as the Irish Olympic Council had not supplied the riders with the requisite Irish team blazers and panama hats, presumably on the cost-cutting basis that you don't supply a second uniform for an already uniformed team!

In relation to Rome, where the Irish performance did not live up to expectations, he explains that they were "competing with untried young horses that possibly weren't quite ready to go to the Olympics; but they all came into their own in 1961 when we had a great year". In that year he was to win the Marseille Grand Prix with *Cill an Fháill* and the Irish Team also took home the Nations Cup from Rome along with numerous other trophies from many high placings with horses such as *Loch an Easpuig*, *Cloyne*, *Loch Garmain*, *Glenamaddy*, *Cluain Meala*, and *Cill an Fháill*.

Promoting the Irish Horse

When the Army and RDS decided in January each year on the countries that should be invited to compete in Dublin for the Aga Khan Trophy in August, it was a calculated and indeed successful marketing venture. The countries whose teams were invited were sure to reciprocate that invitation, and the good name of the Irish horse would be further enhanced abroad, thus helping to promote the Irish horse, the breeder and as a consequence the Irish economy. The Italians in particular had been buying Irish horses for years, so Italy was high on the list and Rome became an annual Army Team trip for five years, an entrancing city which he never tired of visiting.

The Middle East

Shortly after his final International appearance at the RDS in 1965, Eamon was posted to Damascus in Syria to serve with the United Nations peacekeeping mission. The six-day war was ended but that did not mean all hostilities had ceased. It was still pre-Civil War in Beirut. Although the

*Winning the Nations' Cup at Nice in 1961. Bill Ringrose on **Loch an Easpaig**, Sean Daly, **Glenamaddy**, Ned Campion, **Cluain Meala** and Eamon O'Donohue on **Cill an Fháill**.*

*Eamon wins the Grand Prix with **Cill an Fháill** at Marseille in 1961.*

*A final appearance at the RDS in 1965, riding **Carraig Rua**.*

Winning Damascus style. Presented with third prize having come first in a jumping competition!

unarmed force, as a U.N. observation mission, had to patrol the Syrian borders, ensuring no engagements occurred, and they were sometimes strafed from the air, or shot at, it was reasonably quiet and as a bonus it was a family mission and the family were permitted to come and live in Damascus. While here he rode horses and competed in show-jumping and remembers winning a speed class on an Arab horse called *Mazoot*. The trophies on display were enormous, silver cups all, but when the results were called out, our man found himself placed in 3rd position to a rider who happened to be the show's major sponsor, a wealthy local jeweller !

On his return to Ireland in 1969 he got involved in buying and bringing on young horses over the Winter months, selling them on in the Spring, until the market slowed down and practically ceased in 1972 with the outbreak of Foot and Mouth Disease. Another Middle East tour of duty followed, this time to the Lebanon where on this occasion things were much more tense and risky. Back in Ireland, he continued working with horses, but a serious fall at a Hunter Trials in Kinsealy when a horse fell on him and damaged ligaments, and later a horse kick to his knee, called a halt to his riding career. He retired from the Army in 1980 and went to work in the Dáil for twenty years serving as Superintendent of the Houses of the Oireachtas.

Although now retired, Eamon keeps in contact with his colleagues in the Army Equitation School and maintains a keen interest in developments there. He is also extremely pleased that some of his grandchildren now love the ponies as much as he did and having enthusiastically taken up the family reins. They are involved in Pony Clubs and Shows, and are all set to maintain the tradition so ably represented, in another era, by their grandfather.

Chapter 5

Parents, Jack and Teresa Bolger

Bobby Bolger
Connemara Pony Producer and Showman

 onnemara pony territory

The Bolger family house sits on a hill at Derrygimlagh, not far from the boggy landing spot of the Alcock and Brown first non-stop Atlantic flight in 1919. It overlooks a lovely vista of the golden coral beaches of Mannin Bay, with the small island of Ardilaun in the foreground.

Looking north is the peninsula of Errislannon, at one time the biggest Quaker townland in Ireland; now, of its 120 houses, only about 30 are local while the remainder are holiday homes. Nevertheless, the district is Connemara Pony territory, and an active Pony Club meets regularly, where local children learn to care for and ride the native pony. To the south one looks over to the Errismore peninsula, with its expanse of grass-beach commonage, and the sea- side grazing of the Bolger ponies at Bunowen.

Ballyconneely village is the hub of this area of bog, rock, sea, and tiny stone-walled fields against a backdrop of the Connemara peaks, a justly renowned beautiful area. The entire sea-washed area is a rich Connemara pony homeland where the native pony has been born and bred for generations. Bobby Bolger built this house in the early nineteen eighties and went on to make his name as a superb Show man of his home-bred Connemaras over the next 20 years. But as the saying goes, 'it was not from the wind he got it'. His family background had been steeped in the Connemara pony tradition.

Jack Bolger and the Connemara Pony Breeders Society

The Connemara Pony Breeders Society, since it was founded in 1923, has run a Pony Show each year. Starting in 1924 at Roundstone, it gravitated

between Recess, Roundstone, Carna, Clifden and Oughterard and finally settled permanently at the Clifden Showgrounds in 1947.

Jack Bolger of Cashel won the Connemara Stallion Class at the Connemara Pony Show on fourteen occasions between 1932 and 1949, and won the Supreme Championship three times. His son Bobby is proud to show the twenty Royal Dublin Society silver medals currently in the possession of the family at Derrygimlagh. His father had won numerous prizes over the years with his mares, both in Connemara and at the Dublin Horse Show and his silver medal collection remains as testimony to his interest and to his ability and skill at producing ponies to come top of the line at Shows for so many years.

Bobby speaks equally proudly of his mother Theresa who was a skilful weaver and wove her own bolts of tweed, and he remembers with a smile the story told of the occasion when her roll of tweed won first prize at the Show in Carna in 1946 and her profit from the sale of the tweed was greater than Jack's stallion prize-money by one Guinea! An American-born lady whose people came from Leam outside Oughterard, Theresa married Jack Bolger in 1936 and in Oughterard they raised a family of five boys and two girls. Theresa was a noted musician, and on occasion, formed part of a band in the town. She also had an encyclopaedic memory for pony names and their breeding and a fund of common sense. Bobby remembers the pony his father bought from the gypsies, taken out from under the cart for Jack to view. A grand animal, but with only a stub of a

*Connemara **Silver Pearl**, Champion Connemara 1941 and 1943, Cárna, with Jack Bolger.*

*Connemara Stallion **Gil**, 1948, sire of **Carna Bobby**.*

*Jack Bolger and Deirdre Donnelly with **Glen Fanny** at the RDS in the late fifties.*

***Story of Tynagh**, Bobby's favourite pony, being shown in England in 1965.*

docked tail. The inventive Theresa cut some of the white tail off another pony, stitched it on to the stub, plaited it in and off they went to the Show next day where the pony won her class!

It was a stroke of family tragedy that saved Jack Bolger's life and brought him to live in Oughterard. His father had come from Co. Wexford to manage the Bank of Ireland in Eyre Square, where Jack was born. The family had been preparing to emigrate to America in 1911 but Jack's mother became ill and sadly died. The American migration was cancelled and the ship they had booked passage on, 'The Titanic', sailed — on what became it's sad voyage to nowhere — without them. Jack and his brother, Willie, came to live with their two uncles, John and Willie Roe, in Oughterard. Willie Roe was one of the founding members, along with Bartley O'Sullivan and Ml. O'Malley who had paved the way for the setting-up the Connemara Society at the Corrib Hotel in 1923.

Oughterard Memories.
The Roes kept thoroughbred horses and also some ponies at Waterfield in Oughterard, and from an early age Jack worked with the horses, and helped his uncle Willie, who ran the daily horse-drawn passenger coach service each day to Galway. As a boy, Jack also won at Oughterard Pony Races riding the legendary Cannonball in the Farmers Race.

Later, as a young man, Jack, who constantly bought and sold ponies, became a noted stallion-master and stood many Connemara stallions, between 1932 and 1952 Among them were *Noble Star*, *Lavally Rebel, Tiger Gil, Inchgoill Laddie, Silver Pearl, Lavally Noble, Dun Lorenzo, Creganna Winter, Carna Bobby, Tully Lad,*and *Calla Rebel.* The Thoroughbreds, *Little Heaven* and *Winter*, and the Irish Draughts *Skibereen* and *May Boy*, also stood with Jack Bolger, which allowed breeders of

Connemara ponies a wide range of choice as to which stallion should cover their mare. The Society usually choose Jack to manage their stallions for the first few seasons, before they were moved to other custodians around Connemara.

The Roes farmed forty-four level acres in Oughterard and also ran Roes Hotel, across the Owenriff river on the main street, and at that time, it was the main hotel in the town. Bobby grew up on this farm with its cattle, sheep, hens, horses, ponies, cats and dogs and was involved in farm work from as far back as he can remember. He enjoyed growing up in these surroundings in this small town on the fringes of Connemara and speaks highly of Oughterard people, who he says, were known for their particular wry sense of humour and for their unique wit.

The yearling Carna Bobby
In the thirties and forties the Connemara Society, had a policy of buying the colt foals of the good type of mare, with a view to keeping the best and by selective breeding gradually improving the Connemara breed, while passing on the substance and temperament of these mares. In 1946 they placed 10 of these foals on Inchagoill Island, the largest island on Loch Corrib near Oughterard, to avail of the empty acres of winter grazing. They hadn't bargained on the hard winter to come, which in folk memory became known as the twentieth century's Black '47, when the West in particular, was gripped by freezing snow and bitter ice.

The ponies on Inchagoill began to suffer in these severe conditions and what happened next became a story of survival. Jack Bolger and his friend John King, rigged up an old pookaun sailboat, made their way to the island, and rescued the seven surviving colts, loading them on to the boat and sailing with them back to the mainland at Oughterard, a round trip of some eight miles.

*Jack Bolger and Tommy McDonagh at the RDS, early fifties, with the mare **Knollwood** and her colt foal.*

Show Talk! Jack, centre, with Lady de Vesci, Garnet Irwin and his daughter Caroline.

*Jack showing **Heather Mixture of Abbeyleix**, a Supreme Champion in 1966.*

Luckily, the yearling *Carna Bobby*, who was to become perhaps the most influential Connemara sire in later years, was among the seven who survived. He could just as easily have been sold to England at that time as John O'Mahony Meade, an English Connemara breeder who came to Oughterard after World War Two, wanted to buy the colt. Jack advised the Connemara Society against selling this pony which had been gifted to him as part of a package, when he bought two other ponies from an owner who did not want to give a luck-penny, but gave the foal instead. Interestingly, one of the ponies the Meades bought and called *Teresa of Leam* after Jack's wife, was the model for the well-known china figurine of the Connemara pony created in England in the sixties.

Importance of 'Type'

Bobby, a Council Member of the Connemara Society, has strong views on breeding. He stresses that 'type' is the most important attribute that must be retained, and is concerned that breeders may be going away from type With an eye to Performance Testing he agrees that while Performance is necessary, 'it adds a bit' it should not be the only criterion by which to assess the Connemara Pony. Correct conformation is a pre-requisite, and the good ponies in the past, according to him, always had performance, as in the heavy farm-work and racing on the strands on community holidays and days-out.

He likes to see a pony true to type, characterised by an attractive head with large dark eyes set wide apart. The head should be well set on, the neck should have good length of rein, set on a strong deep body with a good forearm and plenty of lung room. Limbs should be straight with good bone, short cannons, a nice round cup-hoof; and the correct type of pony should have above all, a good

temperament and substance combined with quality. This substance comes from the mare, some of the quality from the Thoroughbred blood.

Carna Bobby, popular stallion

Carna Bobby, he claims, was responsible for the most beautiful mares and he also gave speed and athletic ability to his progeny. Like his father Jack before him, Bobby believes that *Carna Bobby* was the result of a covering of *Carna Dolly* by a Thoroughbred sire, and not by *Gil* as is registered in the Stud Book. He believes that because *Carna Dolly* was such a strong substantial mare, she had passed on her native Connemara characteristics to her foals in spite of the extensive Thoroughbred element in her own breeding. With *Carna Bobby* his one conformation weakness showed in his back-end going down to his hocks, a typical Thoroughbred strain in the inheritance.

Arab and Thoroughbred blood

As regards movement, the older ponies had low action, while the Arab blood, when introduced, brought in high action. There were three characteristics resulting from the introduction of Thoroughbred blood: These were a better shoulder, a faster turn of foot, and longer rein, meaning length of neck. A less desirable product was the high rump. He thinks that more Irish Draught blood of the *May Boy* variety, might sometimes have been a better cross than the Thoroughbred. *May Boy* was a small Draught type with great conformation, possibly bred in Aran, who stood with Jack Bolger in the late forties.

He admits that it is hard to breed the consistent Connemara type today because there is so much mingled blood in the breed.

Bolger family at school. Back: Stephen, Robert, John and Gary. Front:Susan, Joanne, Marian and Triona. Missing: Stephanie, Paula and Kevin.

Bobby's daughter Stephanie with mare and foal at Clifden Show.

*Bobby with **Coral Prince** at the RDS. In 1993 Coral Prince took the Supreme Championship at Clifden.*

Favourite Mares

Bobby's advice to breeders is 'look at your mare's type, conformation and temperament, and try where possible to improve on these characteristics'.

He speaks of the mares with pride and affection and stresses that breeders need to get back to the older *Carna Dolly* type. *Carna Dolly* had five foals by the Thoroughbred *Little Heaven*, while that stallion stood with Jack Bolger in Oughterard. She had previously won both the Local Farmer's Race and the Open Pony Race on the same day at Oughterard Races before breeding both *Carna Bobby* and another prodigious racing mare *Cashel Bay*. *Cashel Kate* was another family favourite and she won the Clifden Championship for Jack in 1967. Among mares of this type were *Drimcong Rose* and *Rose of Barna*, while *Gloves Misty* and *Cáilín Ciuin*.also typify this ideal.

Cloonisle Coral Strand by *Abbeyleix Owen* ex *Cloonisle Lady*, one of the more recent mares, foaled in 1988, was said to be the best yearling filly ever with perfect conformation and presence, ie the 'look at me' factor.

The Dedicated Pony Men

Bobby recalls men from all over Connemara bringing their mares to be covered by *Little Heaven* and other stallions that stood, at various times, in Waterfield. The Connemara owners, he says, loved and cared for these ponies best of all. He recalls how a man with a bag or two of food tied to the carrier, would cycle the uneven track all the way from Carna to Oughterard, leading the mare from the heavy bike. The bags contained food, not for the man himself, but for the pony, who was treated to regular feeds of oats to sustain her on the journey back home again the following day, after being covered by the chosen stallion. A round trip of

some sixty miles was not uncommon for these mare owners.

He cites the old Connemara saying 'He thatched his house today, he'll thatch his pony shed tomorrow' as an indication of the important place taken by the working pony on the family farm. The older men, who had to make a living from them, had a lot of knowledge in caring for and treating problems in the ponies. Jack Bolger was known to have had the gift of getting infertile mares to go in foal. He would collect moss on a hillside and weave it into a circular shaped ring; this would be inserted into the vulva of the mare before covering took place, and the previously infertile mare would produce her foal the following year. Co-incidentally, it is nowadays recognised that moss has certain curative and antiseptic properties.

The Carna men in particular, whose families wove their own tweed, had a traditional way of dressing, when bringing their ponies to the R.D.S. in Dublin. The suits, made up by the local tailor, had a distinctive cut to the jacket with inverted pleats at the back, and sometimes plus-four type trousers. Bobby describes Pat Walsh in the 1950s as an example, leading his Connemara mare at the Spring Show in Dublin, dressed in a bright grey tweed suit of this type, different and eye catching,

In the late 1940s, after the War, Jack and Teresa still lived in Oughterard. Jack, in informal partnership with an English woman, Miss Cynthia Spottiswoode, a founder member and the first Secretary of the English Connemara Society, and a Daisy Sadlier from Tipperary, sold many ponies out of Connemara to England, using the contacts of these two ladies. In fact Daisy Sadlier, when her family was selling the home farm in Tipperary, offered Jack Bolger first refusal on the farm. He

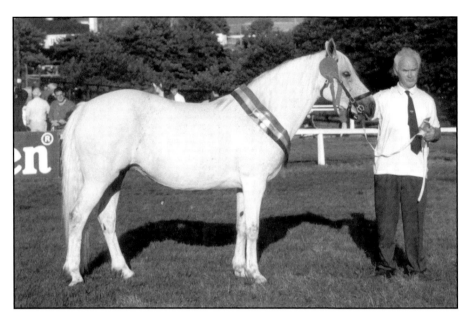

With Clifden Supreme Champion in 1995 and again in 1997, the home-bred mare
Coral Misty *was paraded through the streets of Clifden.*

Queen Gillian, *Clifden Supreme Champion both in 1994 and again in 1999.*

*Bobby's grandson, baby Bobby at the family's
Waterfield Stud in Boston.*

was then out-bid by a certain Vincent O'Brien, who subsequently made this Ballydoyle property the hub of his racing empire

Family move to Cashel in Connemara

Foregoing a move to Tipperary, Jack bought a business for the eldest son Willie, a store and pub, in Cashel, south Connemara, and in 1951 Bobby, with his family, moved away from Oughterard of many memories.

In need of grazing, the family acquired two islands in Cashel Bay, Blue Island was one of these and the Bolger ponies were grazed there. Bobby for a few seasons took part in the 'flapper' races in the area and had a particularly successful racing mare, *Cashel Bay*, one of the progeny of *Little Heaven* and *Carna Dolly*. Bobby paid big money for *Cashel Bay* — ninety pounds was a lot to pay at that time. Father and son concentrated on racing for about six years in the 50s and 60s, travelling to pony races every weekend, up and down the west coast of Ireland and often further afield, often buying and later selling large numbers of foals as future racing ponies.

Story of Tynagh

Another favourite mare, indeed the all time favourite, was *Story of Tynagh*, a six year old chestnut mare by the thoroughbred sire Turbulent. She was bought at Renmore Races for one hundred and forty pounds in 1959, a good buy considering that it was not unheard of for a top racing pony to fetch five thousand pounds, indicating how highly regarded these 'racing machines' were at that time. He raced her all over the west and southwest of the country in the early 60s. She was unbeaten in 14.2 h.h. racing and became All-Ireland Pony Racing Champion.

The Racing days of that era were a big social occasion and combined pony sports such as bicycle racing, musical chairs and potato races as well as children's sports, and when held on the Connemara strands, such as Errismore, or Lettergesh near Tully Cross or Omey or Callowfeenish, currach racing might be held when the tide came in.

Bobby used to ride cross-country in Connemara on *Tynagh* and he now praises her talent and especially her intelligence He describes how one day when the kitchen door was open *Tynagh* managed to glide quietly into the narrow area which held the kitchen dresser, and reverse out as quietly as she had appeared, but now with a loaf of bread in her mouth! 'Enchanting' was how he described this pony and he was not happy to hear, on his return from a sojourn in the U.S., that she had been sold to England. The blow was softened slightly by the knowledge that she was doing extremely well in all disciplines with her new owners. *Story of Tynagh* was a complete all-rounder, excelling in every type of event, whether it was show jumping, point-to-point, or flat-racing, which saw her winning two days in a row in England, a true performance pony.

A New Family

Bobby met and married Bridget Mullan from Ballyconneely in America in 1969 and they returned to Connemara.to settle outside Clifden. He set up as a Builder's Provider, working throughout the whole of Galway west of the Corrib, and he and Bridget raised a large family of eleven children. Although they were never without a Connemara pony, the ponies had to take a back seat for a while as the Bolgers got on with the business of raising a family and making a living.

He started out again with a little dun mare called *Question Time* which he bought with his brother-in-law for his sons to ride. He later acquired *Tessie D.* who subsequently produced *Tessies Colleen* who has been a good breeding mare for the family

Coral Misty's daughter, *Coral Ciara* with her foal in Boston.

Silver Shadow. This young stallion enjoys swimming at this Connemara beach. Photo by Ruth Rogers.

in recent times. Once he had decided to start breeding and showing again, he looked around for the best bloodlines. He bought *Cloonisle* foals from Eoin Reilly of Cashel, each year and when he bought *Cloonisle Coral Strand* who then won the yearling filly class at Clifden in 1989, he knew he had made a good choice. Sold on to England, she proved a prolific winner in performance classes with her delighted owners and her progeny are still topping the line at Connemara Shows in England.

A Decade of Success at Clifden Show. Coral Prince, Queen Gillian, and Coral Misty.

He was now back to Showing with renewed enthusiasm and he made the nineties a decade to remember. He showed ponies for many owners, and remembers showing fourteen ponies in one day at Clifden! With his shock of white hair, he became a familiar figure at Connemara Shows every weekend; a good man to show a pony in-hand, he knew how to get the best performance out of them, he showed them at their best with flair and skill. Clifden became his platform with the RDS in Dublin coming a close second.

In 1990 his home bred mare *Coral Misty* won the Archbishop's Cup.

In '93. *Coral Prince* by *Murphy Rebel* won the Stallion Class, the Confined Championship and the Supreme Championship of the Show.

In '94 *Coral Star* took second place in the stallion class while *Queen Gillian*, whose sire again was *Murphy Rebel*, won her mare class and also the Supreme Championship.

In '95 Bobby brought *Coral Misty* out again and she won both her mare class and the Supreme Championship.

It was a unique achievement, to take the Clifden Supreme Championship three years in a row, with three different ponies all by the same sire *Murphy Rebel*. *Coral Misty* was paraded through Clifden and the party in the Clifden Bay Hotel afterwards was an un-parralled night to remember for Bobby, Bridget and the Bolger family. But more was to follow.

Winter grazing at Bunowen in Connemara.

Bolger Connemaras run free in their native habitat.

In '97, Bobby was to again receive the Supreme Championship trophy, again with the mare *Coral Misty*.

The turn of *Queen Gillian* came once more in 1999, yet again Supreme Champion.

A matchless achievement indeed to take this Trophy five years out of seven. *Queen Gillian* was rated as the best brood mare ever to enter Clifden. Her line is carried on in the U.S by her colt son and in France by a daughter.

In recognition of the Bolger family contribution to improving the Connemara Breed, in 2004 Bobby was chosen as the Connemara Pony Breeders Society recipient of the National Equine Hall of Fame Award at a ceremony in Athlone. This lifetime achievement award recalled many evocative memories of his late father Jack and the many, many Connemara ponies that had passed through the family hands over the past sixty years or more.

Plans, the American Waterfield Stud

Three Bolger sons, Gary, John and Robert, along with Bobby's brother, Clifford, have started another Connemara pony breeding and training venture in Norwood outside Boston and have to date imported eight foundation ponies from their Connemara home to this new U.S. base. The Oughterard link is strong as the American stud is to carry the prefix 'Waterfield'.

Back home, Bobby has plans for a pony heritage museum and an old forge, as he believes it is very important to preserve some knowledge of traditions, customs, and the old ways of doing things before it all becomes a dim memory. The hilltop house, built on the site of an old farmhouse, is surrounded by 'work in progress' as the Bolger plan gets underway.

Some of the trophies won by the Bolger family.

Chapter 6

Mavis Bourns,
Shirley's mother,
in a Hunter Class
at the RDS,
nineteen forties.

Shirley North
All round horse-woman

*S*hirley North,

a remarkably dedicated all-round horse-person, is closely involved with horses virtually every day of her life. Whether she is hunting, eventing, driving, showing, racing, show-jumping, or managing a Pony Club; horses, in one equine guise or another, consume all four seasons of the year for this lady. She has successfully tried all of these activities, excelled in most and above all has hugely enjoyed all work and play with her horses.

Living with her husband John and daughter Sorcha in Kilconnell in East Galway, Shirley is an engaging interviewee, and that mischievous and acute sense of humour that horsey people seem to acquire the longer they are associated with horses, is hers in abundance. Her entire life to date has been lived in the East Galway countryside, that is apart from a few years spent at boarding school outside Dublin, plus a period working in London and visits to her American husband's homeland. She has never wished for any other life and is the first to acknowledge that this life, in which hunting has played a major part, is a privileged one.

Parents and ponies
Shirley's mother Mavis was a skilled horsewoman but father, Tommy Bourns, was not altogether keen for their three children to be involved with horses, perhaps because he had seen his wife suffer some falls on the hunting field. However, resourceful Mavis managed to get around this prohibition one day when a game shoot was being held in the grounds of the family's Lisbeg House near Ballinasloe. When the guests had arrived and just before the shoot got under way, an elderly man, one of the beaters, arrived up the driveway leading an ancient pony from his bicycle. He had of course been organised by Mavis. Her two small

daughters, (Shirley was aged nine) were allowed to ride around on the pony for the day, while her father could only politely ignore them rather than make a scene when the place was full of visitors. After that day's riding there was no stopping Shirley and sister Bill, as their mother had won her point, and ponies and horses were now tolerated, ridden, and loved, round the clock at Lisbeg. Her older sister became known as 'Bill' as it was the closest that toddler Shirley could get to the pronunciation of her given name of Phyllis.

Her Dad actually liked horses and he especially enjoyed the Circus and brought his children, not only to every visiting Circus, but also to the different venues that they played in. This encouraged the Bourns children to start their own circus tricks on the ponies at home in the garden, where they had a wild and hilarious time, only ever seeming to fall off whenever father came to take a look! Her mother, on the other hand, was invariably very casual and free and at home with horses. Shirley remembers that Mavis would often appear out from the kitchen in skirt and apron if she looked out the window and had seen that they needed some help. She would strip off her apron, get up on their pony, in her skirt, and ride it around, to demonstrate to them how certain horseback manoeuvres or movements could be achieved. Of course they teased her about the taking off of the apron and the difference this might make to the pony involved!

Country and farm
Each Autumn for seven years, boarding school at the private Hall School in Monkstown in Dublin, ended the rural idyll. The head-mistress of the Hall School aspired to produce her girls to stand out

Mavis jumps a champion stone wall.

*Shirley aged two, on **Coolcarthy** with mother Mavis and father Tommy Bourns.*

The family home, Lisbeg House.

*Shirley with her first two ponies, **Bo-Peep** and **Mr. Ev.***

from the crowd by their good manners and deportment, to be in fact 'Hallmarked' as she so neatly put it! The saving grace about school was being allowed to go for riding lessons each week to Burton Hall, Ian Dudgeon's riding establishment in Stillorgan.

The two girls returned back home again to the country each summer, where, growing up on a large farm, work, such as driving the horse and cart and helping with the hay, was expected of all family members. The children used their ponies as 'cow-ponies' to herd the cattle and looked for places to jump from field to field. There was also hunting in the winter-time, then as now, Shirley's great passion. Their mother brought them out with the NorthTipperary Hunt, as she herself was from Nenagh. Dogs were also an integral part of life on the sheep and cattle family farm, and Shirley fondly remembers a sheepdog pup she had trained and called *Sweepie*, 'He once jumped out of an upstairs window when I was leaving to ride to a local meet, he trotted the four miles to the meet and when he met the pack he wished the ground would open up and hide him!'

Later, in the seventies when they were known locally as the 'Bourns girls', Shirley and Bill went hunting with the re-formed East Galway Hunt and took part in a lively social scene of Hunt Balls, outings with friends and boyfriends and other party engagements. Shirley's hunting education and work with the hounds at that time taught her: 'to skin animals, to tow a trailer and even to build dry stone walls, which was a necessary skill for putting the country back to right after hunting, and is still a useful skill in Galway'.

Then came a spell working in London in the business end of a cosmetics company, and there she learned to cook, as she says herself, 'in order to entertain.'

She also qualified as a remedial teacher 'in case I had a bad fall which prevented riding to hounds, what would I ever do living in the middle of nowhere?'

Hunting and hunt horses

On her twenty first birthday she received a gift of a mare she called *Dubonnet*, who lived to the great age of thirty six, being with Shirley for thirty three years. She was a great mare to ride over the 'dirty' East Galway Hunt country as she preferred ditches, gates and boggy land to the stone walls of the Blazers territory further west. In fact, according to her owner, *Dubonnet* had an uncanny ability to travel across bogs on the top, and not sink. The mare was a talented jumper and Shirley's brother Richard successfully show-jumped her.

When Dubonnet was retired to stud, her first foal was *Sapphire*. This mare, which is now twenty two, has bred seven foals, all now sold on and doing well in the world of sport horses. Shirley bred and broke all her own horses for hunting, rarely buying in a horse, the exception being the current hunter, *Calvin Klein*, who was found for her by the well-known Willie Leahy, of Aille Trail Rides and of Dartfield House Museum, among other projects. For this horse she is eternally grateful as 'Calvin Klein is the most wonderful hunter, brave and honest'.

Another cherished horse was *Gregory*, who actually loved to jump the stone walls of Blazer country. Partly because of *Gregory's* jumping preferences Shirley moved over to the Blazers early in the 1980's, and for the last eight seasons has been a Joint-Master of this famous County Galway Hunt. Her hunting days have included whipping-in to three different Masters; Michael Higgens, Michael Dempsey and Charlie Bishop.

John Ringling North, centre back, as a clown in the American Ringling Bros. Circus.

John competes a gaited horse in Pitsburg, 1959.

Some family members at Christmas in Lisbeg. Mavis, Richard's wife Deirdre, Bill, Richard and Shirley in rear.

John North

Shirley has hunted regularly with the Galway Blazers for the last 25 years, ever since she and John Ringling North II married and settled down to live at the farm his father had bought near Aughrim. Across these level acres John raises Angus cattle and also enjoys riding around the farm to work the stock on horseback. The hunt horses are used for this job in summer, a custom harking back to the time Shirley and her sister Bill worked this way with their ponies back home at the family farm at Lisbeg.

John had a background in horses as his father was one of the Ringling family who owned the famous American Circus, Ringling Bros. & Barnum and Bailey. The Circus, known as 'The Greatest Show on Earth' and managed by his father, was sold on in 1969. In the U.S. John showed what are called gaited-horses as they have two extra gaits; they will walk, trot and canter and also do what is called a 'slow gait' and a 'rack'. Shirley and John have bred a few racehorses and John has raced as an Amateur. A favourite mare was *Polly Ringling* who was 2nd in a Bumper at Galway Races with John on board. This valuable Thoroughbred bred three colts but they regretfully lost her after a foaling. However they succeeded in getting a pony foster-mother for the day-old foal which survived the trauma and went on, like her dam, to run races

The Joint-Master's job

The Galway Blazers, with Shirley as one of the Joint-Masters, hunt three days a week, meeting sometimes at the kennels in Craughwell or at a country pub or crossroads. The Blazer's hunting countryside is flat and fertile land, laced with stone walls and interspersed with bog and woodland. There is lots of work involved for those organising the hunts, before, during and after the average five hour day spent riding and jumping in all sorts of weather. In addition to Shirley's hunting

responsibilities she is currently caring for six horses and ponies in the original old stables behind the new house, which Shirley and John had built and moved into last year. This means that there are also six stables to muck out each morning, horses to feed and usually up to twelve hay-nets to be filled. Not for the unfit or the faint-hearted, and this is only a prelude to the departure and the hunting day ahead.

The Hunting day

Before leaving home, Shirley gets dressed in her hunting gear, loads the plaited horse, (or two when daughter Sorcha is involved), drives to the meet, tacks up, chats and socialises, welcoming hunt followers until the move-off. The Joint-Masters are basically hunt helpers and there is no financial reward in this, just expense! It is more like 'hunting first class,' according to Shirley, who wears the navy hunt coat (the men wear the scarlet) with its brass embossed buttons, rides up front with the Huntsman, sometimes helps the Whipper-in or takes charge of the hounds, or acts as Field-Master.

Other less predictable duties arise, such as on one memorable occasion, thirty years ago now, when she heard a shout 'Stop the train — hounds on the track'. Shirley waved down the train, which just happened to be the inaugural trip of a new train on the Dublin-Galway route, and was filled to capacity with dignitaries, government ministers and officials. The train driver dutifully stopped his train and an embarrassed Shirley on horseback had to explain to the driver about the hounds blocking the track. She has inevitably suffered a number of falls over the years, although that is thankfully a rare event, and she is usually able to pick herself up, dust herself off and carry on again.

Nowadays, unlike in days gone by when the 'county set' dominated the hunting field, all types of people take part on a regular basis, and

*John North racing **Polly Ringling** to 2nd place in a Galway Races Bumper in 1990.*

Daughter Sorcha , 1990.

*Bill on **Paper Moon** and Shirley on **Martha Murphy**, Horse and Hound 1987. Photo by Jim Meads.*

Sorcha as backstepper hangs on as mother Shirley drives in competition.

Horse and Hound snaps the Galway Blazers in full-cry in Nov. 1986. Photo by Jim Meads.

especially on a Saturday when farmers' children as well as their town cousins, dominate the field. The annual 'children only' hunt around Christmas time is Shirley's charge also and the 2004 event had fifty-five children out riding their ponies for the day.

After the hunt it's back home, clean off the horses, bandage legs, do stables, feed horses and four dogs, make the family dinner, clean coats and tack and polish brass buttons for the next outing. If you didn't love the life this would all be very daunting work indeed, but this lady revels in it. 'My social life and friends are all connected through it, and I think that would be the biggest loss to me if hunting were ever banned in this country. Hunting has shaped my life and outlook on life more than anything'

Farmer goodwill
Not surprisingly, one of the most important duties of Joint Masters is to help keep good relations with the farmers who allow the hunt on their land. Shirley has travelled to London for the pro-hunting Countryside Alliance marches and is an ardent supporter of the continuation of hunting in Ireland; even though 'there have been huge changes in the

countryside, barbed wire and housing developments, and now we are to have the motorways, and still those people hunting enjoy their sport thanks to the farmers' generosity. The only thing that will endanger our sport in this country is if we neglect the farmers by allowing an influx of visitors or by not controlling those who do come out'

And, referring to riders who become impatient waiting around while a covert is checked out by hounds and who might want a day of continuous galloping around, Shirley observes
'Some people would be better to have a 'jolly' around a cross-country course or go on a charity ride if they need instant action; I prefer my sport naturally and Galway is still a huntsman's paradise'.

The Pony Club
On Sundays there is no day of rest as Shirley is currently in her fourth year as District Commissioner with the East Galway Hunt Pony Club, and she consciously gives a lot of time to this job and the children involved. The Club Rallies are normally held at the Showgrounds in Ballinasloe, close to home, but for stable management training,

*Shirley hunting with **Calvin Klein** 1992.*

***Calvin Klein** jumps a tricky barbed-wired wall with Shirley.*

*Colour-coded family trio. Bill on **Batty**, Sorcha on **Joey** and Shirley on **Cleo**. All three horses have on different occasions been taken hunting by young Sorcha.*

*Shirley, Joint Master of the Galway Blazers, with **Gregory**.*

tack maintenance and care, and road safety training, the children travel to their D.C's yard. There are Rallies and Events to organise, and training sessions for activities such as Pony Club Games and Triathlon, which involves riding, running and swimming. Tests must also be organised, while Jumping and Dressage trainings help children to prepare for the many National competitions in which they compete. Shirley also helps to co-ordinate the Pony Club Camp, a highlight of the clubber's summer, when children with ponies can stay for five days away from home at Gurteen Agricultural College. Each day at Camp is organised around instruction and learning to care for their ponies, in addition to taking part in mounted activities. In many ways, Pony Club Camp is a school of horsemanship with a good dollop of fun thrown in.

The world of Showing, mothers and daughters

The showing scene, which takes place mainly at weekends from April to September, is a unique, intriguing and under-researched facet of the equine sporting world.

Although Shirley has always shown horses, her daughter is currently the main showing person in the family and in recent years, a notably successful combination at shows countrywide has been the mother-daughter duo of Shirley and Sorcha North.

In fact they form one of those mother-daughter teams so often observed at Shows throughout Ireland where mother acts as driver, groom and 'gofer' for the day.

Like other dedicated mothers, Shirley helps with schooling, preparing and conditioning the ponies for the event, then drives to the Show, pays the entries and collects numbers and catalogue. She will help the rider tack up, adjust the practice jumps, calm the nerves, watch with bated breath her offspring perform in the ring and either make a mess of things, get placed by the judge or maybe win a class, all the time exchanging chat and pony gossip with friends and acquaintances.

In Shirley's case, there are often three or more ponies in her lorry, some belonging to different owners and all entered in different classes. While Sorcha is performing in one ring, her mother may be observed tacking up a pony for another class, juggling tack around, or hoping one ring will finish in time to enable daughter to take part in a class in another ring. While John, 'my back-up boy', is not usually present at the ringside, he is a major facilitator of all the riding activities of mother and daughter.

Every week you will meet the same people at the Shows, some travelling from far afield while others mainly patronise the local Shows. Sometimes, you will find a father-daughter combination in this game, but generally sons are a rarity in this world.of pony showing and they are, of course, missed, especially by the girls! The competition can be very intense but the spirit of co-operation among competitors is strong. Lasting friendships are formed and children, in the process, learn to lose gracefully as well as win.

Driving

A driving enthusiast of some repute, Shirley got started in this sport when Granny gave a Shetland pony, previously driven, to Sorcha, and a cart and harness was borrowed. Next a Connemara pony was broken to harness and a road cart and new harness purchased. Sorcha, by now, was able to groom, ie stand at the back to help balance the cart and hang on for dear life. This is known as 'backstepping'. The competitive urge had now firmly kicked in and they were soon on the road, competing all over the country and even qualifying

*Hunter Trials with **Rathclough**.*

*Sorcha eventing at Dartfield with Lady Anne Hemphill's **Tulira Katie Daly**, 2004.*

*Sorcha on **Huntington** wears the Irish team green jacket in Working Hunter Championship in England in 04.*

*Sorcha and **Tulira Katie Daly** sport winning rosettes in 03.*

for the National Driving Championships. Not every pony, however, is suited to driving and 'the next acquisition turned out to have a touch of the 'Ben Hur' about him and after a few 'hairy' drives was deemed unsuitable'
So they progressed to a horse by Bill's Thoroughbred stallion; they also bought a Bennington marathon vehicle and a top of the range set of harness, all financed by the sale of one of their home-bred Thoroughbreds.

However, with Sorcha spending more time showing and jumping ponies, the carriage driving 'got put on the back boiler', but only temporarily as Shirley has yet more plans for a four wheeler and more competitive driving in the future. She also hopes to spend more time on her painting hobby now, especially as the new house has been built 'for wonderful light everywhere'.

Sorcha

Sorcha, now a seasoned performer, excels in the field of showing, and among many recent awards gained, the teenager was chosen to ride on a Working Hunter Team representing Ireland in Wales, riding *Huntington*, a striking coloured pony, trained and schooled to a high level, like all the North ponies, by Sorcha herself. On Lady Anne Hemphill's *Tulira Katie Daly*, she has taken the Connemara Ridden Pony world by storm in recent years, having won the top awards in both of the performance championships at the major Connemara Show in Oughterard.

She has also successfully taken *Katie Daly* Eventing and in Hunter Trials. She has made her mark Show jumping, and was also selected as a team member to compete at a British Connemara Pony Society Show in England. In 2004 she competed for, and was awarded a training Bursary by the Irish Pony Society, which she spent with top Show-jumping trainer Ian Fearon as Show-

jumping is the direction she now plans to take.

Although Sorcha has advanced through the ranks and come a long way in pony competition, one of Shirley's most memorable moments was when Sorcha won her first jumping competition at Loughrea Show, aged ten. Shirley remembers that her mother Mavis was dying at the time, and sadly, she recalls that Sorcha's win was 'about the last thing that registered with her'.

Acknowledging how privileged she is to live her personal dream of a life with horses, and with the ponies currently for sale, to be replaced by horses with show-jumping experience for Sorcha, Shirley would dearly love to see her only daughter realise her young dream of competing in a future Olympics. And perhaps she will come 2012, who knows?

*Sorcha and **Tulira Katie Daly** were Supreme Connemara Performance Champions at Oughterard in 2003.*

Chapter 7

The three boys jumped **Greenville Laddie**, this brilliant little pony, Thomas at age twelve won the 128cms. National Championship with 'Laddie' at Dublin Horse Show.

The O'Briens
Show-jumping farm family

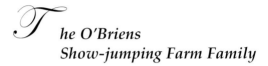

he O'Briens
Show-jumping Farm Family

The O'Brien family of Grange near Athenry in east County Galway have been well known as one of the most outstanding and successful families on the pony Show-jumping circuit in Ireland between 1990 and 2004.

The husband and wife team of Tomás and Frances were both born and reared in this rural area of undulating fertile farmland and are in the process of expanding the equestrian centre behind their modern farmhouse. Starting with two stables in the mid 80s they have built up to twenty four today, housing a varied selection of horses and ponies. Approximately half of the equine tenants are owned by the family and the rest are horses and ponies kept at livery or being trained and brought-on by the O'Briens. A large sand arena containing a course of jumps, a horse walker and sixty five acres of green fields complete the picture. The horse business is now full time, as their milking herd has recently been sold and only the beef cattle remain. An indoor arena is on the cards and for Tomás, who can turn his hand to any building job — having built the family house in 1980 — this will be a hands-on job also.

Farming and Horses
Tomás has always been involved with horses. As a child he remembers his father Joe jumping at Shows throughout the West, specialising in the champion stone wall. This was the high jump competition of that era, and Joe O'Brien travelled on his bike with the horse in tow as far afield as Elphin in Roscommon and Ballinasloe to jump and often win with *Mountain Dew*. Both of Joe's brothers, Tommy and Jack also drove their horses and carts long distances to Oranmore to deliver turf

and collect seaweed for the land. The same farm work-horses took the brothers hunting when the Blazers met locally. Tommy, a successful showjumper, subsequently trained racehorses from 1972 on.

While some of his brothers went pony racing, ponies did not feature in his boyhood years, for Tomás, even then, had one main equestrian interest and that was in the sport of Show-jumping Throughout his life, this has been his sole equine passion, and this same enthusiasm is now firmly ingrained in his own family today.

His own horse
When Tomás was fifteen in 1757, his father bought him his first horse at Ballinasloe Fair. This was *Temple Tynagh*, a two year old well-bred animal which he trained and took Show-jumping, making an auspicious start by winning his first class at his first Show. It was at Bunratty, where he had to beat ninety other horses, but it started him on a track from which he has never since deviated: he was hooked on the sport, as he says himself, 'show-jumping mad' Tomás jumped in Junior Trials and attended trainings in Charlie Haughey's Kinsealy estate with Paul Darragh, Trevor Monson and Emer Haughey under Anthony Paalman and Iris Kellett, although he did not make the team to go abroad.

Sadly, his father died at an early age leaving Tomás, the eldest of twelve, with the responsibility of looking out for his younger siblings. At only nineteen he had to grow up rather quickly and for some years he was kept busy, in his spare time, training his six younger brothers and their horses and driving to Shows throughout Connacht. He

*Tomás taking 2nd place at Ballinasloe Show in 1959 jumping the novice **Temple Tynagh**, his first horse.*

Frances with her father Thomsie Uniake, aboard their farm workhorse.

*Tomás jumping the notably named **Uniake** at Claremorris Show.*

smiles as he remembers that in the early days of lorries without ramps, the driver always had to locate a suitable bank or loading ramp on the roadside, unload and walk the horses to the showgrounds and repeat this procedure, walking back and forth and loading each horse after it had jumped its rounds.

A New Family

Having inherited a family farm, he met and married Frances Uniacke from nearby Dunsandle and they have four children, Joseph, Ruth, Thomas and David. Frances, also raised on a farm, was no newcomer to the world of horses as they always had working horses on the farm. It was only as an adult that she discovered that both her father and grandfather were steeped in the horse tradition, her grandfather having broken and trained young racehorses for Lord French, and her father Thomsie Uniacke having show-jumped as a young man. Both men had also been involved in the Hurling tradition, and had gained treasured Croke Cup medals so obviously hurling, rather than horses, was the main family interest.

Bringing *Temple Tynagh* up the ranks to grade A in show-jumping started a pattern which was to be continued in the present generation of the O'Brien family. The challenge as well as the fun, according to Tomas, lies in buying a complete novice and by training, conditioning and working with the ability of that animal , producing a performer that will continuously improve and compete at top level, either with the O'Briens or with a future owner.

Outstanding among the novice ponies they brought on were *Greenville Laddie* in the 128cms category, *Ballindooley Quee*n and *Rosie Duncan* in the 138cm. section and *Mid West Star* in the 148cm. As well as the brilliant six year old *Bertas Clover*, these ponies were all bought locally and brought up to Grade A level by the family. *Bertas Clover*,

bought as a three year old, is by a *Clover Hill* stallion, *Moores Clover*, who never grew to horse size, and she is out of a Connemara mare. A striking dark bay mare with a strong sturdy frame, she has jumped incredibly well in her short life with her rider David, especially during his last year in ponies.

David and travel abroad

In 2004 alone, the family made four continental trips, competing at six Shows, with the Irish pony Show-jumping Team. Youngest son David acquitted himself admirably, coming 2nd in the individual in Fontainbleu, 3rd in the Grand Prix in Holland and also jumped to victory in Germany where he won an International Class. It was also a year in which the O'Briens made the long sea and overland road journey to compete in Poland at the European Pony Championships, with five team ponies in their lorry.

Another trip to Liege in Belgium and Verona in Italy in November resulted in a Grand Prix win for David and *Bertas Clover* at Liege. This was an incredible win more especially so because the Liege Grand Prix had never been taken by an Irish rider. Furthermore, the breeding of *Bertas Clover* is as Irish as they come, being all Irish Draught and Connemara. Their return to Grange at the end of the last overseas trip of the year when they were nearly three weeks away was especially memorable. The Grand Prix win at Liege was celebrated in style with a big house-party and bonfires along the roadside, an unforgettable welcome home. Another big day was when David aboard *Star of Cashel* broke the Irish pony high jump record, by clearing 1.85 metres at Portlaoise Pony Puissance in 2004. Grandfather Joe O'Brien, a high jump specialist in his own day, would have been proud!

Joseph the eldest son, started jumping **Midwest Star** *when he was eight years old and continued riding him for seven years. He is seen here winning at Verona in 1998.*

Tomás hunting his uncle's horse with the **Blazers** *c. 1986.*

Thomas on **Aille Gille**, *Pony Show-jumping Team at Liege in 2002.*

That was the first year that family commitments had enabled Frances to travel to see the family compete abroad. She was chief navigator in the lorry with Tomás driving the ponies for the Irish pony team, and she enjoyed it hugely, learning to take the twenty minutes of sleep when the opportunity arises, and to live with the inevitable tiredness like a seasoned campaigner. The trips abroad meant weeks away from home, driving five valuable ponies in all sorts of driving conditions, from snow covered mountain roads to busy motorways all over western Europe.

David's schooling was not overlooked as he was flown home after each event to be minded by his grandmother, and to put his head in the books again, preparing for the Junior Cert. Exam. His last year in ponies was to end on a very high note when he was presented with the Irish Field award as Pony Showjumper of that Year.

A great sport, Show-jumping

Frances and Tomás thrive on the life that success in Show-jumping has brought to the family. According to them, their involvement in the sport has meant the children have passed their teenage years trouble-free. Being totally committed to their sport, with equestrian events every weekend, the schooling and preparation of the ponies leaving little time for other diversions, they have, their parents happily claim, been easily reared. They both stress that they and the entire family owe a lot to Show-jumping, a great sport in their view and one of the few sporting activities where both boys and girls can compete at the same level.

For them it is an enjoyable lifestyle, whether winning or losing, trying harder each time, taking on board the responsibilities, the disappointments and the joys, an adrenilin fix each time they compete.

The three O'Brien boys have all represented Ireland on pony teams some eight or nine times abroad, travelling to France, Italy, England, Holland, Germany, Belgium and Poland. They and their sister Ruth all started competitive Show-jumping at age eight, and not before, Tomas being of the belief that children can pick up bad riding habits if they start at a younger age when they are not really able to understand instruction.

Joseph

The eldest, Joseph, started at age eight riding a 148cms. pony called *Mid West Star*, the only pony the family owned at that time, little thinking then that the whole show-jumping affair would take off and reach the heights it has today. The O'Briens then acquired a 128cms. chestnut pony, who was to become a continuing fixture on the circuit for some years. *Greenville Laddie* became the family schoolmaster, and was successfully jumped by each of the younger members of the family in turn. Joseph rode novice ponies for other owners and rode for people all over the country, building up a vast amount of experience and skill in the process. He was the RDS McDonalds Equitation Jumping-class winner in the competition's first year and on the same day took the Red rosette in the BC ponies class with Thomas Welby's *Park Larry*, one of the many Connemaras to pass through the O'Brien yard. On this exciting day he was also placed in the 148cms.Grade A's on his own *Mid West Star*, a pony by the thoroughbred stallion *I'm a Star*, brought from Novice to Grade A by Joseph. With the Irish Pony Team in Le Toquet, this pair were 4th in the Individual and Bronze in the Team. It is also satisfying for the O'Briens, that since being sold on, *Midwest Star* has continued to be a prolific winner for his new owners, having won a Gold Medal winner for England on two occasions.

*David, the youngest boy jumping **Greenville Laddie** at age eight at the RDS.*

*Sponsor Ann Smurfit with Thomas and **Star of Cashel** after they won the National B.C. 148cms. Championship at the RDS. Gaining other kudos, they also represented Ireland at Liege in 2002.*

*Ruth qualified **Park Larry** for the McDonalds Equitation Jumping for the RDS, being congratulated here by owners Mr and Mrs Thomas Welby from Oughterard.*

*David jumping **Rosie Duncan** in 02.*

RDS luck

Each of the previous fourteen years had seen the O'Brien family regularly pack ponies, tack, feed and hay, grooming kits, rugs and mucking-out gear, riding clothes, boots and hats, into their large horse transporter and move to the RDS in Dublin, camping on site for the duration of the five day Show, the highlight of the year for all those involved in this sport. Ruth and Thomas soon joined their older brother on these Dublin trips, having won the necessary qualifiers until the reins finally passed to youngest brother David. All have done spectacularly well, Dublin has been lucky for them.

Thomas

One of Frances's most enduring memories is of seeing Thomas on *Greenville Laddie* jump the winning round in the 128 National Championship competition in the main Arena at the RDS. She had just arrived, rather late and rushed, on the bus from Galway and managed to see him, last to jump, go clear. The pony had been going badly at home and in the Simmonscourt competitions earlier in the week, so she felt such a great surge of joy that the tears came, and when asked by visiting Americans onlookers beside her if she knew this boy and his pony, she cried out 'yes, he's mine' It's a moment she will never forget. Thomas, a couple of years later, went on to win the 148 BC's at Dublin and was the recipient of the same honour at Millstreet that year. In 2002 he represented Ireland on the Irish Pony team at Liege, coming through with *Aille Gille*, owned by Willie Leahy of Aille Cross, as the best of the Irish competitors.

Both Joseph and Thomas had received International Burseries from the Show-jumping Association of Ireland. Joseph spent his with Eric Lavellois in Northern France and Thomas, the youngest ever recipient at seventeen, spent his with Billy Twoomey in England.

Ruth

Ruth, the only daughter, also made a reputation for herself in pony jumping , mainly at local Shows, but on *Castle Ellen* she has also been the winner of a coveted Dublin qualifier. She also qualified the striking chestnut Connemara, *Park Larry* for the McDonalds Equitation Jumping in the RDS. Currently, hunting is her main love, which she manages to fit in while working and studying as a 3rd year student nurse in Castlebar.

The Lifestyle

Taking pride of place in the 'feel good' section of Tomás senior's mind has been the memory of listening to the playing of the National Anthem, overseas and far from home, when one of his family had won or been placed in a competition.

About winning he says he has always stressed to his family that 'how you ride is more important than winning' while admitting that winning is the main motivation that has kept them interested and enthusiastic. He knows that the younger rider needs a school-master pony to take him or her round a course of jumps and thus avoid the discouragement that can easily take hold when a novice rider is trying to steer an inexperienced or second-rate pony round a jumping track. Yet he himself has never bought a top pony for any of the children. All were young novice ponies which Tomás bought locally and which the family took great satisfaction in bringing to the top level in Show-jumping.

Tomás as Pony Producer

When owners bring ponies to him for training he will give them his opinion of their abilities in no uncertain terms, either telling them not to waste money on a loser or offering to train that pony where he sees potential as a jumper. An uncanny judge of a young pony's ability and potential, he is a past-master at producing his ponies to reach the

*Taking things easy at Galway Show. Thomas, **Rosie Duncan**, father Tomás and David.*

*An important part of every jumping competition, Thomas puts studs in **Rosie Duncan's** shoes to guard against slipping.*

top and his experienced judgement has almost always paid off. Up at 7.30 each morning, he works seven days a week, schooling, preparing, bringing on and producing show-jumpers. For him it's not just about getting over a challenging fence that counts, but how the animal is going and to this end when training he will spend hours working on the flat and jumping grids or lines of low fences, as well as the usual lunge work.

A local man, Martin, works with him on the stable management side and between them they get through a large amount of stable work, exercising horses and schooling, with Tomás riding to correct any problems the animals might display, before the boys get home each afternoon from school in nearby Athenry. Both parents are adamant that, whatever about the jumping, education has always come first, so homework was first item on the agenda each evening for the family during their school years. Then they would school ponies and horses outdoors, under lights in the shorter days of the year, and prepare for the competitions, which take place every weekend, right through the year.

The human-horse partnership-a way of life

The sport and all it entails, the donkey work, the good days when they win and the disappointing days when they go badly, has become a way of life for the O'Briens, and one they would not ask to change. Over the years friendships have been built up with like-minded enthusiasts and going to a Show to compete is also a social occasion where the same people congregate, catch up on news and watch the competition jump, whether in a local indoor school or at the colourful arenas of the bigger Shows in the RDS or on the European circuit. The tension and apprehension, which instantly evaporates with the joy at achieving a clear round, and above all the satisfaction, on a good day, when rider and horse have gone well together, more than makes up for all the hard work behind the scenes at home. The O'Briens bring to their Show-jumping a quiet and professional style which makes even a high and complex jumping-track look smooth and effortless. They would probably laugh at the notion, but to see them compete is to experience the sensation of excellence in this human-equine partnership.

The move into horses, Joseph and Thomas

Joseph, Thomas and more recently, David, have moved into the horse ranks, again with considerable success. Riding Jimmy Flynn's horse *Heather Cruise*, Thomas took the 1.20 metres Young Rider's Award at the RDS in 2003 while this pair also took the Munster Championships, in both the 1.10 and 1.20 horse classes against the professionals. In 2004 Joseph qualified to jump in the Grand Prix at the Galway County Show where he jumped a clear first round with his French bred *Icarus d'Aravan*. A story his mother tells of Joseph, her eldest, gives some clue as to the nature of the driving enthusiasm that keeps these young riders going. Currently completing his final year in manufacturing engineering at Galway Mayo Institute of Technology, in late summer the twenty-two year old student broke his leg, not while jumping his horse, as might be expected, but while playing in a hurling match. With his leg encased in plaster, albeit covered by a black stocking, and with the permission of the authorities, he insisted on competing as he had always done, this time in the Inter-Varsity jumping competitions. Later, based in

*David competes **Star of Cashel** in Holland in 04. With this pony they broke the Irish Pony High Jump record.*

***Bertas Clover**, a prodigious 148cms.jumping pony seen here with David in Poland. As a young six year old this combination won numerous awards, both at home and representing Ireland abroad.*

***Bertas Clover** winning at Millstreet in 2004.*

*Joseph jumping his horse **Icarus d'Aravan** in 2004.*

Holland for the final leg of his course, he wasn't long there before he managed to contact and got involved with the famous VDL stud.

Tomás is totally positive about the family transition to horses from ponies. He admits that while he enjoyed working with the ponies down through the pony years with the children, horses are what he really likes. Over the last Christmas period, with all the family, plus young friends, home full-time, they had eight young horses in the yard, ready to start work. Amidst the fun and festivities of the Christmas season all eight horses were backed and ridden before schools and colleges re-opened. This is his life and he loves it!

Parents Tomás and Frances at an indoor Winter jumping event at Glenamaddy.

Chapter 8

Visitors to a lesson at Knockranny in the hills above Moycullen 1983

Judy Cazabon
Riding Centre

$\mathcal{J}$udy Cazabon

It is quite an experience to enter the Cazabon family home in Cleggan, especially if you choose a busy day in Summertime. Here in this old square stone building, formerly the schoolmaster's house, you are likely to meet three if not four generations of this family at any one time, plus various 'horsey' visitor, a riding instructor or two, all happily drinking tea or milling around, and of course, director of operations and 'mater familias', Judy herself.

A Galwegian since the age of one, Trinidadian born Judy and her partner, local man Enda Keane, are responsible for the Cleggan Riding Centre which they have worked to build up over the last ten years. The Centre specialises, particularly in the summer months, in providing the ultimate Connemara experience for visitors from all over the world, who arrive to view the spectacular local scenery in the best possible way, from the back of a locally bred, sure-footed and safe Connemara pony.

Family background
One may wonder how a woman of her exotic background came to settle in this Connacht outpost. One answer lies in her fascination with horses and ponies, since the times as a child when she was taken horse riding by her mother to the Athenry establishment of brothers Chris and Eugene Daly. Here, mother Yvonne and small daughter took lessons together and rode out weekly in the fields, forestry and quiet roads of the east Galway countryside. Judy fell for the whole scene in a big way and grew to love the horse environment she experienced there; the yard, the horses and especially their smell which she remembers trying to retain on her hands

afterwards, not wanting to even wash these horse-smelling hands! There and then she decided this was the life she wanted for herself when she grew up.

Her Trinidadian father Roy, who had booked to study medicine at University College, Galway, arrived with his young family in 1956. The plan then was to return after qualifying as a doctor, to work back home in Trinidad. However, as the Cazabon family expanded and schooling soon became an important issue, the plan to return home was abandoned and Dr. Roy has worked as a Surgeon in Ireland ever since. In their home in Galway, Judy heard him talk of the horses ridden by his grandfather, a cocoa plantation owner in Trinidad, who always rode around the estate on horseback. This made her even more unwavering in her decision to follow her chosen career path. Horses, as they say, were 'in the blood.'

Family, and Riding School in Moycullen
Marriage at an early age, the move to Moycullen village outside Galway and the birth of her three children put Judy's plan on hold for a number of years. As soon as the children had started school, this decisive lady took action. Each morning she donned her motorbike gear and roared off on her Honda 50 motor-bike on the 20 mile round trip to Rockmount Riding Centre on the far side of Galway, to work for her instructor's qualification to teach riding. Her departure and arrival home was timed to fit in with the children's school times.

After several training visits to Iris Kellett's riding establishment in Kill, Co. Kildare, this aim was achieved. Judy was now a qualified Instructor and without delay she managed to borrow a few ponies

A lesson at Knockranny

Trekking at Cashel, 1988.

*Siobhán winning with **Mervyn Blue Tack** at Clifden in 1992.*

from friendly neighbours in the Moycullen area. She then roped off a corner of a hilly field beside the house and advertised her riding lessons.

With no business plan or financial backing, she was just a young woman raising her family but her determination to work with the ponies she loved, and make her living from this work, was a burning motivation. She was now up-and-running and an outdoor sand arena was built, followed soon after by a spacious indoor Arena on the Moycullen site.

A fresh start

Family circumstances, including a break-up of her marriage, later necessitated a move to Cashel in south Connemara. in 1988. With the help of friends and family, (she had hurridly left Moycullen 'with nothing but the children'), she soon managed to move her horses and tack etc. to Cashel where she had found a small cottage and 50 acres to rent. Here yet again, in this rugged but scenic south Connemara terrain overlooking Cashel Bay, she managed to build stables and a riding arena, and with the help of the children, Eleanor, Siobhan and Roy, ponies, lessons and organised trekking again took over. Niece Danielle came to work with the ponies every summer and is now an accomplished showing rider and still part of the team.

'One of the nice things I remember from those days is the numbers of children and teenagers I used to teach in Moycullen, coming all the way out to Cashel for lessons and staying a few days or weeks. They had their favourite ponies and were not willing to give up on them. The house was a tiny three- bed cottage but on any night during the summer months you could count up to 15 heads. It was like a summer-long pony camp and I would not have managed without the help of my children at that time. That summer I met my present partner. Enda, although a fisherman, has a great affinity

with horses and has been a great help to us over the years.'

She also ran actual official Pony Camps there for children in summer. The children stayed in local houses, and there were always friends and pony - people coming to ride, help out and sample the hospitality of Judy and her family in the old cottage kitchen of the hillside house. Enda's two daughters, Rachel and Karen, also became part of the family and have often been depended on to lend a helping hand.

Pony Shows and Sucesses

Having enjoyed showing her ponies it was inevitable that she was instrumental in organising Pony Shows in Cashel for a few years running and also at Cleggan.

Judy had been involved in Showing since she acquired a Connemara foal in the early days living in Moycullen. That filly foal was a progeny of the famous stallion *Carna Bobby*, and was one of the last surviving foals by this popular sire. As *Drimcong Rose*, she was to win many mare classes, over twenty in all, at Connemara shows over many summers. 'Rosie' also worked for her keep in the riding school, and still lives out her retirement, hale and hearty in Moycullen, where she has produced a number of foals, some of which were sold on to France. Now thirty years old, she shares this peaceful retirement with another much loved mare *Mervyn Blue Tack*, a winner of ridden classes both at Clifden in 1992 and the old Dublin Spring Show in the early 1990s. She was later shown successfully by Siobhan as a top in-hand pony in her teens, winning many valued prizes in her showing heyday.

A trek down country lanes near Cleggan.

A canter on Cleggan strand.

'Coloured' ponies as extras in film 'The Field'. Sisters Eleanor and Siobhán.

Draíocht na Mara *and Judy receive the Brennan Supreme Championship Cup at Galway from Ann Brennan.*

Lisglassick Laura was another familiar pony at earlier shows, winning the ridden class twice at Clifden and at twenty one years of age producing her first foal, the prolific winner of recent years, *Draíocht na Mara*. The gelding *Aran Andy* was yet another Dublin success, taking second and first prizes in two successive years in the Young Ridden Connemara class. *Andy* won the first Kity O'Shea Championship at the RDS, and went on to compete successfully in England.

On the move again

The move in the early-nineties came about when the opportunity arose to use a field owned by Enda in the Cleggan area and give clients an experience many of them wished for, that is beach riding. Initially the riding operation was carried out in these two centres, about thirty miles apart, 'taking beginners in Cashel where we had an enclosed arena and taking the more experienced riders in Cleggan where we had some of the nicest beaches in Connemara, including Omey Strand, on our doorstep'.

They maintained a caravan at the Cleggan site to house some enthusiastic young trek- leaders each summer, but finally a house in Cleggan was purchased and the 'build up the business' work started again. To the stables and sand arena were soon added the tack shop and the office, colourfully decorated by the many rosettes won by the family at Shows throughout the country. The business expansion continues to this day as plans for an indoor school are finalised and it is hoped to start the building work in the near future.

Trekking worries

The work of running the Riding Centre is never-ending as ponies and horses will always be a seven-day- a -week affair. From St. Patrick's day on, the busy season is upon them and each day is a trekking day. Even though every rider is assessed in the sand arena before going out on a trek with experienced leaders, Judy worries about each and every group until they arrive back safely again, knowing that, reliable as the ponies are, you never know when one animal may just 'have a bad day' Thankfully this would be an extremely rare occurrence, but you can never forget that they are after all, just animals.

The Showing Season

While Judy especially enjoys her teaching, and the Riding Centre world of ponies that she can care for and call her own, the Showing Season each year continues to be the icing on the Cazabon cake. She and daughter Siobhán between them thrive on the whole Showing experience, starting from early in the year with the conditioning and the training of the ponies, to eventually producing them in top form and top condition in the Ring. The satisfaction is obviously more complete when one of their own home-bred Connemara ponies does well. Most of her showing ponies are bred from her own mares. *Lislassick Laura* who produced *Draíocht na Mara* also produced *Taibhse na Mara*, another successful ridden pony.

Cú na Mara, yet another prizewinning gelding, is out of *Mervyn Blue Tack*, the Showing star for the family in the ninetees.. Siobhán in recent years has often taken the honours at many Shows around the country, with *Draíocht na Mara*, including Clifden in particular and the Dublin Horse Show where the pair were recently in the Reserve slot in the Kitty O'Shea Championship.

One year at the Dublin Horse Show stands out for both Judy and Siobhan, when all three of their ponies shone. That year, 1997, was the year of the three firsts, for *Draíocht na Mara* in-hand as a four year old mare, for *Aran Andy* in the ridden class and for *Mervyn Blue Tack* in her mare class.

Four generations of Cazabons. Back: Judy and her son Roy. Front: Siobhán's daughter Alana, Judy's parents Roy and Yvonne, and Siobhan's son, James.

Side-saddle winners, Siobhán and **Draíocht na Mara**.

Alana and **Baby Face** in a Lead Rein Class with Siobhán

Siobhán and Scarlet take the Ridden Hunter Class at Galway County Show.

Enda with horse and carriage, wedding duty at Station House Hotel, Clifden.

For the Cazabon family it was as though all their Christmases and Birthdays had come together.

Even the long road trips from their Connemara outpost to Shows all over the country are no deterrent and Enda and herself are well used to driving the pony lorry lengthy journeys over narrow bumpy roads. Their ponies have been remarkably successful, and the many rosettes and trophies decorating the tack shop they run, attest to this. At Shows in the last couple of years, it has not been unusual to see three generations of her family compete, Judy usually riding or showing a mare in hand, Siobhan competing in the ridden classes and Alana, Siobhán's daughter, being led on the lead rein on her small pony *Baby Face*.

Irish Names for Connemara Ponies

Judy is atypical among breeders in choosing Irish names for her Connemaras. Strangely enough it was rare for pony men, even in the vast tracts of Irish speaking areas, to give Irish names to their ponies. Perhaps if was felt that an English name was a better selling proposition, but whatever the reason, it just wasn't part of the Connemara tradition. Coming from a non-Irish background and not stymied by tradition, Judy was more than happy to use the Irish names as proposed by Enda. Broadening Horizons.

Broadening Horizons

Judy and Enda are ever open to diversification. Enda, as well as being a salmon fisherman, also drives a variety of carriages and gigs. He has his own small collection of driving horses and carriages, including a brougham, a phaeton, a side-car and various tub-traps and gigs, which are hired out for weddings and film work. Driving one or other of these, he can be seen leading the St. Patrick's Day Parade in Clifden each year. He is a member of Carriage Driving Ireland and has

worked on numerous films all over the country, driving all sorts of vehicles.

Dog Training is yet another of Judy's activities. 'I have been horsemaster / animal wrangler, on several films, supplying riders, horses, donkeys and dogs, even sheep, cattle, chickens etc. We both really enjoy the film work, even though the hours are long it is usually great fun'. Spot them in 'Tristan and Isolde' and 'Waiting for Dublin'. Family members also had fun with their roles as extras in 'The Field' and the ponies used in the shooting of that film, painted with makeup to become 'coloured' ponies, were from the Cleggan Centre.

Family involvement

Daughter Eleanor and son Roy, who always worked as part of the family team in the early trekking days in Cashel, have now gone their separate ways, but two of Eleanor's small children are already 'into the ponies' when they visit Cleggan. Siobhan's small children are growing up surrounded by ponies so it seems reasonably certain that Grandma Judy will see the family well represented in the Showing rings of the future.

However, it is middle daughter Siobhán who seems to have inherited the equine passion from her mother, in that she has chosen to be involved professionally with the ponies on a full-time basis. Siobhán wears a number of equine hats and all of them are pony linked. As well as working in the Riding School, training young horses and ponies and helping out at the Connemara Pony Club at nearby Errislannon, Siobhán, with husband John, is bringing up their two small children.

She also finds the time for her job at the Connemara National Park where she is responsible for the welfare and care of the resident Connemara

Children happily display their rosettes at the Riding Centre.

***Draíocht na Mara** and Siobhán receive the Kitty O'Shea Reserve Ridden Connemara Championship from sponsor Kevin Loughney and Judge Nicola Musgrave at the RDS in 2004.*

Trekkers from the Riding Centre make their way back from Omey Island at low tide.

Pony herd and gives introductory talks and information on the ponies to visitors to the Park at Letterfrack during the Summer tourist season.

Future Plans

Judy was never one to put her feet up and say 'this will do'. This determined woman is now in the process of planning for the building of the brand new indoor school at the Cleggan Centre. Lessons can then of course be organised, ponies schooled, and events run, in all sorts of weather and life will be a little easier, (and drier!) for all concerned.

A recent trip to the United States will have given the members of a Pennsylvania Pony Club the unique experience of being taught by an Irish-Trinidadian Instructor from Connemara during their week long Pony Club Camp this year. Perhaps this will be the start of a new and positive trend of international pony co-operation with a diversity of new riding styles and skills being brought back and forth across the Atlantic. Who can tell?

One thing is clear; whatever other new venture this woman from Trinidad comes up with, she'll go for it heart and soul and without a doubt, make waves!

Riding back from Omey.

Chapter 9

*Tommy O'Brien and **Ballybrit** take a fence at the RDS, in the mid-sixties. On Monty Clare Tommy had a win at the Dublin venue and they also took a Championship in Cork.*

Val O'Brien
National Hunt trainer

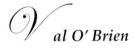 *al O' Brien*

laughs at the very notion that he might have done something else with his life. Why would he? The job he is doing, bringing on potential 'chasers, is what he loves best and finds most satisfying, and there is no way that he might have chosen another career or lifestyle.

A quiet unassuming man of middle age, trainer Val O'Brien gives the impression that he would not easily be fussed or perturbed when things might go wrong with his young horses in training. He is in calm command of his Galway establishment, in the countryside of his forefathers near Athenry, where his word is law.

Morning time — the O'Brien Yard
On a cold, grey March morning he is preparing to travel some young four year olds to Thurles for a few races the following day. The surrounding stone-walled countryside, far from awakening to its springtime splendour, is suffering the effects of persistent cold northerly winds and belated winter frosts. Recently grazed limestone fields have that scalped and dry grey look, as though the grass has decided to retreat into the cold ground rather then burst forth to meet the expected warmth generally brought about by the longer days of Spring.

But at least it is dry under foot and when six horses and riders come around the bend of the six-furlong all-weather gallop, life and colour dramatically re-enters the scene. The horses are shining, fit and well conditioned and are being systematically prepared for a Summer season of racing. The young work riders bring the horses out walking on the road to cool off, then return, untack, rug up, water and feed their charges before immediately tacking up the next six horses, which have already been warmed up in the horse-walker for their training session on the gallop.

With thirty-five young horses currently in the yard for training and six or seven young people working with them, this is a busy training centre. April through to October is the most demanding time when travelling to Race meetings countrywide a couple of times each week becomes the norm. Between April and October the yard team will be on the move weekly, travelling two, three or four horses to any one of twenty six race-courses around the country. Val was happy enough with the racing year 2004, which was a good year for the O'Brien Yard as they clocked up seven wins and quite a few seconds.

Father, Tommy O'Brien
Val himself has been bred to a seven day working week since he first went show-jumping with his father Tommy, a well known and successful show-jumper in the sixties and early seventies. Tommy, who bred, backed and brought on most of their notable horses, first made his mark in the world of show-jumping, before turning his attentions to the racetrack. His son recalls the day Tommy jumped *Monty Clare* to a championship at Cork show and also another occasion when he took a Red ribbon with this horse at the RDS.

At that time the family lived on Galway's College Road where they kept horses at the nearby stables attached to the Sportsgrounds. These stables, now long demolished, used to house horses arriving for the Galway Races by train, which were then led up the length of College Road from the railway station. The grounds were the venue since 1942 for

Val taking the Wills Premeir Steeplechase at Haydock in England with **Leap Frog**

Val winning the Novice Chase, Galway Races, with **Tubs** *in 1971. The home-bred Tubs won 12 races in all for the family including the Ulster National and he also finished 11th in Aintree.*

the Galway Horse and Agricultural Show, and many competing horses and ponies were stabled here for the duration of the two-day Show, but this event faded out in the late nineteen fifties. Tommy was a Committee member in 1966 and was a driving force in the revival of the Show here in that year, after a seven year gap. Tommy and his four sons kept five or six horses stabled here, which were produced for show-jumping and later for racing, by the family.

Val works for Trainer Tom Dreaper

In the sixties Val worked for eight years as a jockey for Tom Dreaper who trained about forty horses at his yard in Killsallaghan in North Co.Dublin. He had his first win at Leopardstown in 1967 riding *Gala Day*, and kept the momentum going with a string of winners both in Ireland and England. The best, most memorable moment of his career came in the Wills Premier 'Chase at Haydock Park in 1971 when he 'sailed home to his expected triumph' (Horse and Hound Jan 22, 1971) jumping *Leap Frog* to his first English victory for Tom Dreaper and owner R.K Mellon. Of his 'brilliant' win Horse and Hound commented

'Having your first ride in England on a red-hot favourite in an extremely valuable semi-novice steeplechase with twelve runners can never at the best of times be anything but nervous work. To his eternal credit, however, O'Brien showed not the slightest sign of haste or anxiety'.

The writer Cornelius Lysaght goes on to say that

'his steadiness under fire' will be tested as never before at the upcoming Cheltenham Festival..... but for this horse all things are possible'

Two months later *Leap Frog* was to achieve a near miss in the Cheltenham Gold Cup when he came second to *L'Escargot* in this prestigious race.

A crashing fall

Unfortunately the same *Leap Frog* that gave Val his first thrilling win was also to give him a far less thrilling moment one year later. This was a crashing fall five out, his worst fall ever, in the Gold Cup at Cheltenham. He suffered a number of fractures due to the fall plus a huge disappointment as *Leap Frog* had been fancied for this race, and here was his jockey, spending a week in hospital instead! So much for the ups and downs of the racing game!

Tubs, the home-bred hero

On the positive side of things, Tom Dreaper was always a good man to work for and Val enjoyed his eight years there as a stable jockey. Along with his many racing wins, he gained. a considerable variety of racing experience. Val still rode for his father while working in the Dreaper yard and the family achieved fame with the home-bred *Tubs* who won twelve races for the O'Briens, including the Ulster National. With *Tubs*, they travelled to England where Val completed the testing Liverpool course to take eleventh place in the Aintree Grand National. Listed among the best race-horses he has ridden, after *Leap Frog* comes another 'chaser, *Good Review* and also *Final Tub*, who was even better than his half-brother *Tubs*, and who won the Bank of Ireland race three years running at Galway Races.

A move from College Road

By the early nineteen seventies Tommy O'Brien was training full-time for jump-racing and the family had moved out to the countryside at Grange in East Galway, near to the old family farm, where Tommy had been raised. There he built a bungalow and twelve stables on a green field site with sixty-five acres. Val recalls the totally rural environment then, with electricity still to come to the area, while today he points out a wide sweep of land where new houses are cropping up overnight and the

*Val and the fancied **Leap Frog** had an unlucky fall in the Cheltenham Gold Cup in 1972. They had come 2nd to **l'Escargot** in the previous year.*

***Half Barrell** with Derek Kelly winning a Hurdle race at Navan*

*Val with **Final Tub** and Son Tommy then aged four. **Final Tub** won the Bank of Ireland race at the Galway Festival three years running*

sounds of construction have replaced the still quietness of those early days.

Tommy died suddenly in 1985 while attending Roscommon races and Val, the youngest of four brothers, having spent a couple of years with his brother Sean in the transport business, took over his father's training yard. Sean, who also breeds a few horses, is now involved working with Val in the yard.

Training at the O'Brien Yard

Over the years Val has developed his own routine of training and assessing the young horses. In the Autumn the three year olds are started and are given six weeks of lunging and long-reining before being backed. They are then assessed and if found to be talented enough they will be raced from early the following year. Promising young horses are brought to the Tipperary racecourse for training gallops over the early Winter months and will start to race in February and March. If some are found wanting — and this is the part of his job Val finds difficult — 'owners must be informed that unfortunately they haven't a swan' and that sending their horse racing (which has been the owners dearly held objective and dream since their horse was foaled) would be a pointless exercise.

An alternative that is sometimes successfully tried is to give the horse another year to mature and this may happen, as big horses especially, develop and muscle up as a four or five year old and both speed and jumping ability increases. Jump horses will generally mature later and have a longer working life than their flat- racing counterparts and it is not unusual for them to go on racing into their teens. They would normally be at their peak around seven or eight. One of Val's best horses in recent years has been the exceptional *Half-Barrell*, winner of twelve races between the age of seven and twelve, including a 'Chase in Galway at the age of eleven.

A number of brood-mares are always kept on the farm and currently these are four in number. The twenty-three year old chestnut mare *Araybean*, a member of the *Tubs* family and dam of *Half-Barrell*, is in foal to *Luther* this year and Val is hoping she will produce a filly to carry on the *Tubs* family line.

Yard routine and the Staff

From 8am to sometime after noon, the young horses are ridden out in groups of six and are either schooled on the gallop or jumped in the sand arena. Val's current staff includes Head Lass Lorna who also holds a jockeys licence, three other girls, Maddie, Ruth and Karen and two boys, Mark and Valdecio who hails from Brazil. After the intensive riding-out of the mornings, in the afternoons time is given to the schooling and assessing of the younger horses, ascertaining their ability and deciding whether or not they are sufficiently mature to race.

Afternoons

In the afternoons, as well as training the young horses, the entire yard is also busy with clearing stables, carting in fresh loads of shavings, checking, sorting and cleaning tack, grooming horses and setting fair. That means leaving the horses rugged for the night, with stable skipped out and with access to hay and water. The farrier attends on a regular basis as there is always work shoeing and caring for the feet of these future stars of the turf. Regular contact is also kept with the vet.

These young people are learning the ropes of preparing, training and conditioning horses for racing as well as getting a grasp of the Turf Club rules and regulations such as the 'how-to' of entering a horse for a race. They also learn the hard fact that many of the horses in training will not

*Tommy proudly poses with **Half Barrell** who won the Tony O'Malley Hunt Chase at Galway with Ruby Walsh on board in 2001. Photo by Healy Racing.*

HALF BARRELL
Winner: *Tony O'Malley Memorial Handicap Chase*
Owner, Trainer and Breeder: **V. T. O'Brien.**
Jockey: **Ruby Walsh**.
GALWAY 3RD AUGUST 2001 (Healy Pic)

Two work riders head back to the O'Brien Yard

make it to the race track, but if there is a good pedigree, that is, with winners in the back breeding, they will be sent on the breeding route instead. Others will be sold on as hunting horses or as Point-to-Point runners or, as a last sad resort, to the canning factory.

Race-Day preparations and decisions

Vals wife, Bernadette, who holds down a job outside the centre, helps out in the yard as well. The thrice daily feeding is a major operation where many hands are needed and Bernie also does the necessary pre-race paperwork. Val himself will usually go on the computer using Mini-tel, the racing information programme supplied by the Turf Club, to do the race entries. This programme gives information on every racetrack in the country, the runners in each race and the type of horse a particular track will suit. As Bernie says 'there are, in actual fact, believe it or not, 'horses for courses'. Val praises the present up-dating which has been carried out at most of the racetracks, with improved facilities for horses and trainers and new stands for the comfort of owners and spectators, which is a vast improvement on his early days in the game. The trainer will then make decisions on which of his horses will suit the track for the next race meeting, and who should ride the horses. He must remember to have his entries in six days before a race and must contact race officials before 10am the previous day to declare the horse. Failure to do this means your horse might arrive at the chosen racecourse and be refused permission to run, and no excuses accepted!

Balloting-out,

A recently introduced procedure, balloting out, is something that can happen at any time: for instance for a recent Fairyhouse race, they had one hundred and fifty eight entries, of which only twenty five were accepted to run. Trainers horses are balloted out in rotation to make the system fairer, but the prodedure certainly adds to the trainer's pre-race anxiety.

National Hunt and Point-to-Point

In National Hunt Racing entry fees to most races is set at 1% of the total race prize money, 8000 being the lowest while at the top end of the scale at some of the larger tracks, up to 150,000 is on offer. Point to Point racing is steeplechasing for amateurs and serves as a training ground for National Hunt, with many well-known jockeys, owners and trainers, as well as horses, receiving their first taste of racing from Point to Points. Horses must carry a Hunter's Certificate and no horse that has won a race under Rules of Racing is eligible to run in Point to Points. Pointing is organised throughout the country by local hunt committees between January and June, is run under the regulations of the Irish National Hunt Society and is usually well sponsored by local businesses. The races are run over about three miles with varied numbers of steeplechase fences. The prize fund is generally close to 1000 with an entry fee of 30.

Uncertainties of the game

The O'Brien premises is a medium-sized racing yard, and is the largest in County Galway, while Val is one of six or seven other trainers in the Western area. As he has made a reputation as a good starter of young horses, giving ample time to their training, owners from all parts of the country bring horses to his Galway Yard. Making a living is not easy at times and the old cliché of digging a hole in the ground into which you are pouring money is one he agrees with. But he enjoys the work and the satisfaction of bringing on young horses and it is very evident that he likes to be in daily contact with these horses.

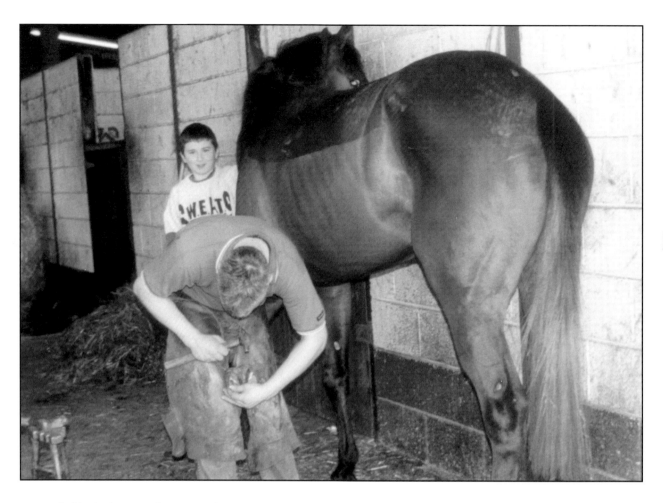

Tommy holds the horse as farrier T.J. from Mallow fits a shoe

Val O'Brien at home

To the outsider, the whole training-racing scene seems fraught with uncertainties; the major uncertainty at all times, winter or summer, being the state of the weather which in turn determines ground conditions and suitability for racing. Trainers in particular have to develop a certain mindset and a philosophy to cope with the many uncertainties involved in their business. The only sure certainty seems to be the continuation of the production of thoroughbreds for all types of horse-racing and the ever-increasing supply of racing fans to support them.

A Third Generation

Val's young son Tommy, now aged thirteen, is actively involved in helping with the horses in the yard, and travels to most of the race meetings when school allows. Tommy has big plans to take his pony on the pony-racing circuit soon. He intends to call him 'The Sundance Kid' so watch out for this pair!

His younger sisters Valerie and Clara will usually be at the local race meetings with their mother, and they too, like Tommy, will obviously get more involved with their father's horses when they are older.

Already young Tommy sees a future for himself following in Val's footsteps, and at the moment he is the family member most likely to carry on this all-consuming interest in the training and running of racehorses into the third generation of O'Briens.

Head lass Lorna work riding

Lorna winning a class with her Connemara stallion **Maxwell***.*

Winning the Ladies Bumper at Tralee with **Lucagene** *in 2004 . Photo by Healy Racing.*

Lorna Murphy
Lady Amateur Rider

 orna

Lorna has been working with Val O'Brien for the past three and a half years and gets immense satisfaction from working the young horses, both in the yard and on the race-track. Now in her mid twenties, she is licensed to ride both flat and jump races and has had over twenty National Hunt and fourteen Point to Point rides to her name.

The way this girl can juggle her commitments is beyond belief. She leads an incredibly busy life as she is also (concurrently) a Law student at the National University of Ireland in Galway, due to sit for her 'finals' this year, and planning to apply for Blackhall Place next Spring and further Law studies for two more years.

The legal-minded jockey

Lorna and the other lads and lasses work at the O'Brien yard from 8 am to 4.30 pm on average six days a week and when Lorna goes race riding, this usually becomes seven days for her. Normally they will take horses to race meetings once or twice a week, although in Summer, their busiest time, this increases to three or four weekly trips. Her lectures take place between 5 pm and 8 pm each evening and she still has to find time to study and sleep!

There is always plenty of work to do in the general training of young horses, combined with cleaning up of horses, stables and yard at O'Brien's, but there is a good working atmosphere in this Yard and that makes a big difference to all concerned. There is no set allocation of horses to each staff member but all of the people working there share the workload, with five or six horses on average

being looked after by each of them. As this is a busy yard with plenty of new young horses coming in to be broken and backed, there is plenty of work to keep everyone active on a fulltime basis.

Lorna enjoys working for Val O'Brien whom she describes as very fair, an easy-going trainer, who, while speaking his mind and telling it straight still manages to leave the staff to get on with their work without undue prompting or interference on his part. Nowadays, girls, who have been permitted to ride in open competitions since 1974, are becoming a lot more visible on racetracks, as both grooms and jockeys. There are about one hundred girls in Ireland holding licences to race although some of these never ride a race.

Background in horses

With a background in Connemara ponies and hunting, Lorna was well rehearsed to enter the racing scene. Many in the Pony showing scene will remember Lorna successfully showing her mother Beatrice's home-bred Connemara stallion *Gleann Rua Maxwell* to win red rosettes in both ridden and in-hand classes at Clifden and Dublin Horse Shows. *Maxwell*, impeccably schooled by Lorna, also took the Performance Championship at Oughterard Show some years ago. After school she moved on to work in a Galway Blazers hunting yard at Craughwell and spent some time working with Trainer Pauline Gavin. By now the racing bug had truly settled in her system and she moved to the larger yard of Val O'Brien where she has since worked and has taken out her Jockey's Licence with the Turf Club for both flat and jump racing.

The Tralee trophy. Photo by Healy Racing.

*Jumping **There's No Doubt** to win the Ladies Race at the Blazers Point to Point in 2005*

A first win and a first fall

In Tralee, her boat came in when she had her first win in the Ladies Bumper, riding Deirdre Connor's horse *Lucagene*, an experience she describes as the greatest achievement in her life so far. Plenty of placings and some other wins have come her way since that day in Tralee, but none of course can compare to her memorable first win.

Lorna took her first fall, a seriously bad one, at her first ride in a bumper at Fairyhouse, when her horse slipped on the flat. She lay concussed on the track for a full half hour and spent a week recovering in hospital. However, this unfortunate experience is now very much put to the back of her mind and has proved to be no deterrent to her ambition to pursue her race-riding career. More recently her determined riding has seen her take the winner's spot in the parade ring at the Galway Blazers Point-to-Point near Athenry.

This win she describes as 'fantastic, I couldn't believe it'. She had just beaten the champion Point-to-Point lady jockey into second place on an incredibly wet and windy country course, and she stood beside her horse, covered in mud yet nevertheless beaming from ear to ear.

Lorna loves the Pointing scene especially for it's informality and friendliness and prefers jump racing to flat racing as 'in jumping there is much more of an adrenalin rush going down to a jump at speed'. In a later race that day she was to have a fall, but no injury, as 'there was a pretty soft landing with the condition of the ground'.

May all her landings in her future legal career be equally soft!

16   Lorna and **There's No Doubt** *with winning trainer and McGrath family connections at Blazers April Point to Point near Athenry*

Chapter 10

Maura Hardiman's grandfather, Matt Francis on **Charlie** in 1932, the only farmer in Rahoon who ever rode a horse

Hardiman Family, City Centre

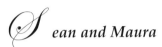ean and Maura

Although he grew up as a country lad on his father's small farm near Corrandulla, some miles north-east of Galway, Sean Hardiman, with his wife Maura and their five children, has spent the major part of his life living within a stone's throw of Eyre Square and the City Centre. Here the family now run a guest-house and are lucky enough to have a small area of land around the house. In the nineteen seventies, eighties and right up to the mid nineties, they kept and trained ponies here.

Secret garden
Their daughter Marjorie describes it as 'wonderful, and for the children it was like having a secret garden in the middle of town'. From here they sometimes went riding 'up the dyke' on the green area beside the river, or prepared the ponies for jumping leagues at the weekend or for trips to Shows in the summer months. When grass was in short supply for the ponies in town they always had the back-up of the grazing at Sean's family farm at Corrandulla. In latter years, amid the noise and traffic of an expanding city and in the shadow of the massive Corrib Centre which rose up and dominated the skyscape close by, they still kept the ponies here, long enough for the first grandchild to enjoy and ride. If you peered out from an upper floor of the multi-storey car park in the early days of the Shopping Centre, you might have spied their four stables, and perhaps a couple of ponies serenely nibbling grass in the railed paddock at the rear of the house.

Woodquay and Horses
Work horses and ponies and carts would traditionally have been kept in Woodquay, as in other areas of Galway, right up to the nineteen fifties, in outhouses and yards at the rear of people's houses. Maura Hardiman's parents were no exception to this custom in Galway's pre-motorised days. There was a close family link with horse-riding in Maura's family, as she has an old picture of her grandfather, Matt Francis, who farmed at Rahoon, on board his working horse. The story goes that he was unique among local farmers in that area at the time for enjoying horse-riding. Maura's mother returned from the United States, married in Galway and the family home at Hidden Valley was built in the space of six months in 1936 just after the closure of the railway line which ran quite close to the front of the house.

The Galway Clifden railway line
A prominent feature of the Woodquay landscape then would have been the very recently disused tunnel and railway embankment of the railway line, which was closed in 1935 after forty years in operation during which Connemara and Clifden were opened up to Galway people and visitors alike. This part of Woodquay is known in Galway as Hidden Valley, as it was bounded on one side by the steep Prospect Hill and on the other side by the river Corrib.

During the construction of the Galway-Clifden railway line in the eighteen nineties, there was a gigantic building site located here, providing much needed relief work in a time of poverty and mass unemployment. Large numbers of men and boys would have earned their meagre wages in the days before machines took over such heavy building work. Horses were the principal means of hauling the work materials of earth, rock, gravel and steel and all materials necessary for this huge building project. From the opening of the Galway-Oughterard line in 1895 and its eventual extension

*Malachy Hardiman on family pony **Pepsi**, a two year old in 1975*

Mal leads sister Marjorie on Pepsi at their first Show together

*Marjorie and Connemara pony **Pat Angus** at Ballinrobe Show in 1983.*

*Mal with **Brucdy Lucky** won pony races at Oughterard and Clifden in 1980.*

Maura and Sean Hardiman celebrate son Peadar's wedding in 1994.

to Clifden, until this massive feat of engineering was closed down and when the tracks and over twenty eight major bridges were dismantled, the steam train chugged back and forth each day through this tunnel within sight and sound of the residents of Woodquay.

Railway closure, horses again

Forty years later, the line was deemed uneconomic and unsafe: it was eventually little used and having been allowed by its owners to run down, it was finally scrapped. At a time when the majority of the population was without motor transport, this must have proved a great hindrance to travel and the horse-drawn vehicle would remain the commonest means of transport for some years to come.

First ponies

Sean's interest in horses and ponies began before he owned either type of four-footed animal, when back in the 1960s he helped out at the annual Galway Horse Show at College Road, just because he liked to be around horses. His first 'hands on' involvement with ponies began in 1975 when three wild young Connemara ponies landed on his doorstep in part payment for a job of work he had done. According to daughter Marjorie, her mother Maura 'had a fit'. What was the family going to do with these unhandled young animals, straight in from the mountain and too big for the children to ride at the time?

A pony-owning friend, Billy Horan, helped solve this problem by driving with Sean to Gort Mart to sell off the Connemaras and in exchange, a small Welsh two year old which caught the eye, was brought home to St. Bridget's Place. This was *Pepsi*, still alive and well today, having been the family pony ridden by all the Hardiman children in

their introduction to the Show Ring. *Pepsi*, was usually brought each spring to be covered by *Kiltinane Charles*, a well known Welsh stallion belonging to the late Gus Keane in Tipperary, and was to produce half a dozen more small show ponies for the family over the years.

These ponies, *Popa Smurf*, *Lilliputian Enchanter*, *Lady*, *Daria* and *Smarty Pants*, as Sean is happy to acknowledge, cost nothing more than their covering fee yet were regular winners in lead rein and small ridden pony classes at Shows around the country over the years, often being preferred by judges to the many similar small show-ponies which had been purchased for substantial sums both in Ireland and England.

Riding, Jumping and Pony Club

The two boys, Peadar and Malachy, from the age of ten, jumped at leagues in Rockmount and Claremorris, on a 13.2 pony named *Burgundy* and progressed to bigger ponies which included two Connemaras, *Local Girl* and *King of the Hills*, show-jumping them at all the local Shows. They were also involved in Pony Club, which was run by Lady Anne Hemphill at her home, Tulira Castle, where there was an annual summer camp for Pony Club members held in the castle grounds.

Sean always had a particular respect for the native pony, especially since his sons had acquired and jumped a talented Connemara pony, *Pat Angus* in the early eighties. This pony excelled in both show-jumping and in ridden classes and took a first prize in both the RDS and Clifden ridden class in 1983 with Mal riding.

Becoming involved in the Pony Club in the early eighties Sean soon became District Commissioner

Warbonnet and Rachel take the red rosette at Corandulla. With Judges Gus Keane and Josie Owens.

Marjorie leads one of **Pepsi's** sons **Smarty Pants** with niece Emma on board.

Shauna and Kevin Finneran won rosettes at Claregalway Show riding **Rathnaleen Spideog** and **Smarty Pants**.

Growing grandchildren, Shaun, Kevin and Emma Finneran.

Kevin and granny Maura mind ponies between classes at a Show.

of the Mid-county branch. He organised many activities for Galway children and their ponies for about ten years, including Pony Club camps at the Ballybrit racetrack premises and he also regularly drove lorries of ponies to Pony Club activites elsewhere in the country. In recognition of his services to the Pony Club he was honoured with a Carew award in 1993. Driving Connemara ponies to the RDS for the Connemara Pony Breeders Society was another regular driving job, and as a listed cattle judge, he was often on the road again at weekends as he drove to judge at many Agricultural Shows.

A narrow escape

Long distance driving was second nature to a man who had driven cattle for a living for many years throughout Ireland, North and South, and especially in troubled times when the Northern conflict was at its height. He regularly passed through the Killeen border custom post, and well remembers the time it was blown up in the seventies just one short hour after he had driven through with a load of cattle on his way to the port at Larne. Later, in another bombing incident, the custom post at Newry, which he regularly drove through, also took the life of the official manning the post, a kindly man who had often offered the hospitality of a cup of tea to waiting lorry drivers.

He continued driving because it was his living but the fear at the time within his own family in Galway was always felt in the background.

The Irish Pony Society

At this time Sean was also deeply involved in the Galway County Show and in Corrandulla where he chaired the annual Show for a number of years. He became the main mover in starting a Western Branch of the Irish Pony Society in Galway and chaired this organisation for over twelve years. During this time many shows in the West affiliated to the Irish Pony Society Classes, raising standards all around. The growth in membership of the Society was due in great part to the unstinting level of energy contributed by Sean who also served on the Pony Society Council for many years.

New Connemara Championships

Sean has for many years been a supporter of the Connemara pony, but in recent years he had felt that our native pony was not accorded any special recognition within the IPS, so he set out to remedy this situation. Along with some like-minded pony people he secured a sponsor for the running of performance classes for Connemara ponies, under the aegis of the Western Area IPS. These Working Hunter and Ridden classes, for riders both under and over sixteen years of age, have been running successfully for a number of years.

His work on behalf of children and their ponies and his love for horses in general has been passed on to the two sons and three daughters of the family. Currently it is the female side which has taken up the reins, in particular daughter Marjorie and grand-daughter Shauna.

Gypsy Gold with Marjorie clears the log at the Riding Clubs Hunter Trials at Gurteen College in Tipperary.

A happy couple, Mark and Marjorie won the Novice Pairs at Lough Cutra Hunter Trials.

Mark with Misty won the Heavyweight Hunter class at Ardrahan Show in 2000.

The Riding Club Generation, Marjorie and Mark

Just off the Oramore-Clarenbridge road, Marjorie and her husband Mark have constructed, behind their newly built house, an equestrian centre that any horse enthusiast would give their right arm for. Looking out over the surrounding farmland they can see over to the remains of the tower house of Creganna castle nearby while in the far distance, the imposing ruins of old Tyrone House stand visible against the skyline.

A shared interest

They both share the same hobby and are equally smitten by their horses as is plain to see from the horse-centred environment they have created here. Having bought the land some years previously before land prices in the area spiralled, they lived for two and a half years in a mobile home on the site while constructing, firstly, the well-planned housing for the horses before finally building their own house. In the large country style kitchen, Marjorie has linked old and new, as the focal point is a large black, shiny, nineteen thirties stove, which her grandmother had installed in her newly built Woodquay family home and which Marjorie had the foresight to save from a shed at the back of that house where it lay unused for many years.

Four of the horses in residence are kept here at livery by their owners, who, like Marjorie and Mark, are Riding Club members. The centre is a model of its kind with bright airy stables, an immaculately maintained tack room, well fenced paddocks, kept clean by the special vacuum equipment for this job, newly planted trees and shrubs and of course the all-important animals. As well as about ten horses, the animals in this horse-farm cum animal-sanctuary include seven cats and three dogs (all rescued) a pair of Muscovy ducks and a trio of hens, all maintained in specially constructed compounds.   Mark, a proficient handyman, who holds down a city job by day, and rides his horse *Black Jack* most evenings, is responsible for a lot of the building and fencing and upkeep of the property.

Irish Riding Clubs

Both are active members and keen participants in many of the Spring and Autumn Show-jumping Leagues, Hunter Trials and Dressage competitions organised by the Association of Irish Riding Clubs in their own region and throughout the country. This Association, the fastest growing equine organisation in the country, was started in 1973 and *'aims to encourage riding as a sport and recreation, to promote good fellowship among riders'*, in other words to provide both fun and education for people who felt a need for horses in their lives but were not prepared to engage competitively in the professional end of the equine sporting world.

Today there are 121 Clubs with about 3000 members in eight regions. The minimum age for membership is 17 years and there is no upper limit! You don't need to own a horse to join and there are competitions for young and veteran horses and even veteran riders!

Marjorie has had many Show-jumping successes on their family-bred *Gypsy Gold*, who is out of their Connemara racing mare, *Lucky* and by an Irish Draught stallion, *The Conquerer*, and she and Mark were happy winners of a Novice Pairs event at Lough Cutra in 2003.   But whatever about winning, according to Marjorie, the main emphasis will always be on fun. Mark and *Black Jack* too have won quite a few ribbons in both Show-jumping and Dressage. *Black Jack* has a Danish warm-blood crown brand on his rump as he was bred in that country for Dressage, but has also carried Mark to win competitions such as the Riding Clubs advanced Intermediate Show-

Riding Club members at Castlebar. Monica Kenny, Suzanne Hogan, Liam Dilleen and Michael Brosnan. Seated, Marjorie and Mark.

An evening water-ride at Rusheen Bay. Mark, Shauna , Monica, Claire and Suzy.

jumping. *Jack* had been the replacement horse bought by Mark when the much-loved grey hunter, *Misty*, was lost on the vet's operating table some years previously.

Resident Horses 'not for sale'

They will never sell *Jack* and the same applies to all their own horses and ponies, as Marjorie unequivocally states, 'we don't sell-off animals from here'. Older ponies and horses are allowed to slip into gentle retirement, but their most senior inhabitant, the thirty year old *Pepsi*, will make a new début this year as Marjorie, who rode *Pepsi* in Lead Reins many years ago, is looking forward to leading their four year old daughter Jane around the ring on the old family pet in a Lead Rein class this summer.

For Marjorie the most satisfying experience in her dealings with horses was the re-generation of a retired race-horse, bought by a friend in France where he had been destined for the canning factory. He was rescued and brought to Ireland and his new Irish owner brought him to Creganna where photos taken after his arrival showed a gaunt, depressed looking animal. Marjorie took on the rehabilitation job of *Christchurch*, this horse that was unable to even canter a circle or bend, and after a year and a half of regular schooling and good feeding, she had a recovered and capable Dressage horse. The fine looking Thoroughbred in its rug, munching away contentedly in the paddock, now at the age of fifteen is visible testimony to the treatment and attention received from someone who cares enough about horses to make this difference.

Shauna and **Smarty Pants** *competing in the RDS Working Hunter competition.*

The Third Generation and Dressage

The Association calling itself 'Dressage Ireland' has been a potent influence in the young life of Sean and Maura's eldest grandchild, Shauna Finneran. Parents Eleanor and Bernard are surprised at this turn of events as there was no previous history of Dressage involvement in the family; Bernard himself had jumped ponies as a youngster and still claims he knows very little about the discipline taken up by their eldest girl..

When she was barely fifteen, Shauna had chalked up respectable wins in the Dressage world, had been selected as a member of the Irish Pony Dressage team and has been part of a major Dressage demonstration in the RDS Main Arena in Ballsbridge riding her aunt Marjorie's Connemara *Milford Sirocco*. Shauna loves riding Sirocco whom she describes as quiet and easy to work with and a pony that, like Shauna herself, is still learning. Together they gave a notable performance in Cavan two years ago which left them in overall second place in the prestigious Silver Spurs Awards Final. The Silver Spurs was quite a difficult test of precision and riding skills especially when the three finalists in the ride-off had to ride each of the other two ponies as well as their own in contention for the main prize.

The Training commitment

Shauna was first introduced to Dressage on her 128cms pony *Robin*, when visiting Marjorie and Mark while they were taking lessons from Trainer Vida Tansey whom they unanimously describe as 'tops' for direction and training. She has continued weekly lessons with her Trainer as well as accepting an invitation to attend for monthly Trainings at Marlton Stud in Co. Wicklow, organised by Dressage Ireland for the purpose of training potential future Irish Pony Dressage team members. Here ten or twelve youngsters who have demonstrated a commitment to Dressage are given individual lessons over the Winter weekends by top Irish International Dressage rider, Anna Merveldt Steffens.

These monthly trips, consisting of a ten-hour return journey by car, two overnight guesthouse stays, plus payment for the lessons, are quite a strain on the pocket as well as being a disruption affecting the weekend activities of younger family members. There is an element of sacrifice involved to get Shauna to Marlton, but because of the interest and support she receives, they consider these monthly trainings well worth while.

Bernard refers to the encouragement from all concerned in Dressage Ireland, who, in the last three years, have brought about a revolution in the Dressage world in Ireland, and he is pleased with what he calls the new 'culture swing' where children from around the country with aptitude are taken on board by the society and given every assistance in an equine discipline previously mainly dominated by adult riders. Another Galway girl, Caitriona Murphy was also on a Team which went to Scotland for a week to participate in the International under 21 Championships which were held outside Edinburgh, where co-incidentally and most appropriately, the five Irish Pony Team members all rode grey Connemara ponies.

Dressage, the 'quiet' discipline

Eleanor describes the Dressage scene as being very different to the Showing scene with which they are very familiar. At the average Horse or Agricultural show where their three children might be competing in half a dozen classes there is normally lots of dashing between rings and getting children and ponies ready. Dressage Shows, on the other hand, are especially quiet. Naturally you do not talk while the Tests are going on, and everything is more subdued and hassle free, with a certain serenity prevailing. Dressage can at times be boring to watch for the uninitiated but is very hard work for the participants, as Shauna will testify. Dressage to music is something which both parents and daughter love and which they describe as 'magic'.

Shauna, if she chooses to stay with the discipline, has two more years in which she can ride her ponies in Dressage. After that she will be into Juniors and will be riding horses until the age of eighteen when she can progress to Young Riders and compete until she is twenty-one. Then the world of Adult Dressage bekons.

At the moment it looks fairly certain that she will continue to follow this path, while still continuing with her jumping and other equestrian activities and perhaps we will see her one day join the ranks of Irish Dressage stars of the future.

*Shauna and the Connemara pony **Milford Sirocco** in 2004.*